Nellie Bly

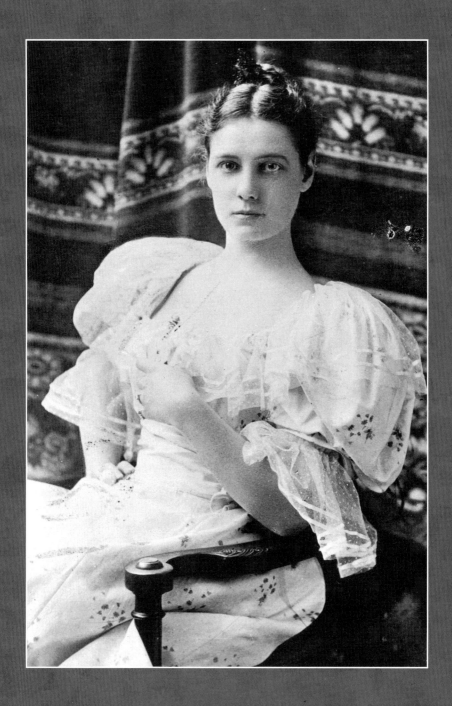

A LERNER BIOGRAPHY

Nellie Bly

DAREDEVIL REPORTER

CHARLES FREDEEN

 LERNER PUBLICATIONS COMPANY • MINNEAPOLIS

For Kerry—the best research assistant ever

My special thanks go to a few people who gave great help in making Nellie Bly come to life for readers, including, perhaps, some feisty future journalists. To the Carnegie Library of Pittsburgh; Dr. Mark M. Brown; Gar Willets; Ellie Temple; Karen Chernyaev, for all her input and support; Brooke Kroeger, for her excellent and inspirational work on Nellie Bly; and my editor, Sara Saetre, for her advice, help, and guidance—thanks all.

Lerner Publications Company
A Division of Lerner Publishing Group
241 First Avenue North
Minneapolis, MN 55401 U.S.A.

Web site: www.lernerbooks.com

Library of Congress Cataloging-in-Publication Data

Fredeen, Charles 1956–
    Nellie Bly : daredevil reporter / Charles Fredeen.
        p. cm.
    Includes bibliographical references (p.) and index.
    Summary: A biography of the woman who helped pioneer
"stunt"reporting at the turn of the century.
    ISBN 0-8225-4956-5 (alk. paper)
    1. Bly, Nellie, 1864–1922—Juvenile literature. 2. Journalists—
United States—Biography—Juvenile literature. [1. Bly, Nellie,
1864–1922. 2. Journalists. 3. Women—Biography.] I. Title.
PN4874.C59F74   2000
070'.92—dc21
    [b]   98-50519

Manufactured in the United States of America
1 2 3 4 5 6 – JR – 05 04 03 02 01 00

Contents

Striking workers in Chicago set fire to railroad cars during the Pullman strike in 1894.

ONE

Misery with Hope

1894

In July 1894, a young reporter named Nellie Bly stepped off a train that had just arrived from New York City in Chicago, Illinois, a city that for the moment resembled a war zone. Thousands of state and federal troops roamed the streets, acting almost like an occupying army. They had been summoned by President Grover Cleveland to control a massive strike by workers against the Pullman Palace Car Company and its owner, George Mortimer Pullman. Bly had come to Chicago to see firsthand what was happening between the strikers and George Pullman.

The United States in 1894 was weighed down by a deepening recession. Like other wealthy industrialists, George Pullman faced declining profits. Pullman had enjoyed enormous earnings in previous years on the manufacture of his luxury railway sleeping cars, known as Pullman cars. Even so, he wasn't about to underwrite the shortfalls caused by the current recession. Instead, he had laid off hundreds of workers and slashed wages for those who remained on the job. At the same time, he had not reduced the generous salaries and bonuses he had been paying to the executive officers of his company.

Outraged, Pullman employees had begun the strike by disengaging Pullman cars from trains and pulling the cars off the tracks. The American Railway Union, led by its president, Eugene V. Debs, quickly joined the protest. Pullman cars were connected to almost every train in the country. The strike spread nationwide as union members in city after city refused to move trains. Passengers, goods, and the U.S. mail were grounded; the nation's economy careened to a halt.

Since the national security depended on rail transport, a court injunction ordered the trains to move. Company owners hired "strikebreakers" to replace striking workers, but strikers massed on the tracks to block the trains. State and federal troops moved in to enforce the injunction. With tensions high, it was almost inevitable that violence would erupt.

It did. On July 4, 1894, strikers overturned some freight cars and set them on fire. On July 5, ten thousand strikers marched on railroad property and set fire to more freight cars. Skirmishes broke out between strikers and soldiers, with injuries on both sides. On July 7, the Illinois National Guard fired into a crowd, killing at least four strikers and wounding twenty.

This scene was an odd setting for a female journalist in turn-of-the-century America. Women were considered delicate, in need of protection from unpleasantness. American newspapers were filled with lurid headlines advertising stories of bloody strikes, macabre tragedies, and political corruption. Such sensational stories were not proper fare for lady reporters. But Nellie Bly was the famous "stunt" reporter who had sped around the world in record-breaking time. She wasn't about to let conventional wisdom keep her away.

Bly worked for the *New York World,* the country's most popular daily newspaper. Most major newspapers portrayed the strikers as inciting the violence in Chicago. Like many other reporters, Bly was "bitterly set against the strikers," as she wrote later. Still, she was determined to learn more about the men and women who were giving up their pay to strike. She wanted the story behind the story.

Once in Chicago, Bly set out for the nearby town of Pullman. Pullman was a "company" town, owned by Pullman Palace Car. First hiring preference at the company went to applicants who agreed to move into the town. Would-be employees who didn't wish to live in Pullman, went the message, could forget about being hired.

Supposedly created as a "model" community, the town, according to a company brochure, was a place where "all that is ugly and discordant . . . is eliminated, and all that inspires to self-respect is generously provided." Bly "thought the inhabitants . . . hadn't a reason on earth to complain," as she wrote. "With this belief I visited the town, intending in my articles to denounce the riotous and bloodthirsty strikers."

However prejudiced she might have been, Bly had a remarkable ability to establish rapport with people she interviewed. And in fact, the people of Pullman gladly opened their doors and hearts to her. They showed her the tiny rooms they lived in. Bly saw that people enjoyed little privacy. Many families shared a single faucet for water, and those living in upstairs apartments had to walk through the downstairs apartments of their neighbors in order to enter their homes. George Pullman had not reduced the high rents he charged his employees for this inadequate housing, even though he had slashed their wages. Pullman expected his town to make profits on everything from rents to water used.

Bly began looking for details to "humanize" her story and found a man sitting on the stoop outside his apartment. He spoke to Bly with a heavy English accent. Bly asked the man, who had "bushy hair and whiskers and the bluest of blue eyes," if there were any poor people living there. He led Bly up "two flights of filthy stairs, crowded with dirty children." A woman inside the apartment was nursing a baby. She half rose to greet Bly and motioned Bly to sit. The man spoke. "If you know anyone as 'ave an old pair of shoes to give away, miss, I should mind 'aving them," he told Bly. "And I'm sure I can't be telling where the children will get any clothes."

Sitting in the impoverished room, Bly asked, "Why did you strike? Didn't you know it would bring misery to you and your family?" The man replied that union organizers had left the workers with little choice. And at least the union made sure his family got food.

Talking to many of the people in Pullman, Bly found that, like the blue-eyed man, most had been opposed to a strike. One woman, as Bly told her readers, put it this way: "Strikes do no good. The poor man is the only one to suffer."

Bly wrote three lengthy articles for the *World* during her time in Illinois. While other reporters across the country railed against the union and focused on real, or sometimes imagined, violence caused by the strikers, Bly's stories were different. She was the only reporter to tell the Pullman story from the point of view of the strikers. The strikers "are not firebrands; they are not murderers and rioters; they are not Anarchists," she wrote. "They are quiet, peaceful men who have suffered beneath the heel of the most heartless coward it has ever been my misfortune to hear of."

Bly was also the only reporter to tell the story from the Bly point of view. Her stories always ran under her byline—

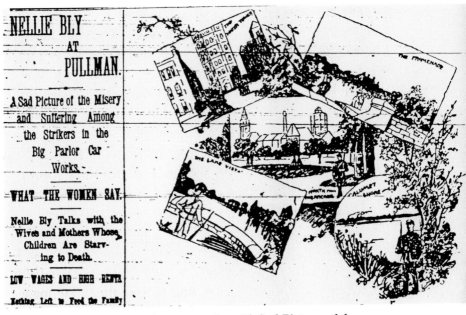

NELLIE BLY AT PULLMAN.

A Sad Picture of the Misery and Suffering Among the Strikers in the Big Parlor Car Works.

WHAT THE WOMEN SAY.

Nellie Bly Talks with the Wives and Mothers Whose Children Are Starving to Death.

LOW WAGES AND HIGH RENTS.

Nothing Left to Feed the Family

This article by Nellie Bly gave readers "A Sad Picture of the Misery and Suffering Among the Strikers." It also told "What the Women Say."

her name. That was an unusual distinction. Bly referred to herself often in her articles, making her own impulsive, sympathetic reactions a central part of the story. "Before I had been half a day in Pullman," she wrote, "I was the most bitter striker in town."

That strong statement, in many ways, was typical Bly reportage. Throughout a career that spanned continents, made international headlines, and championed popular and unpopular causes alike, Bly never was one to let a moment of drama slip by.

Nellie Bly's real name was Elizabeth Cochran. Her father built this spacious home in Apollo, Pennsylvania, when she was five years old.

TWO

In the Beginning

1864–1879

The spunky young woman who so identified with the downtrodden Pullman workers began life in comfort, the daughter of a man of wealth and stature. Bly was born on May 5, 1864, in Cochran's Mills, Pennsylvania. Her parents named their newborn daughter Elizabeth Jane Cochran.

Tiny Elizabeth joined a large and still growing family. Her father, Michael Cochran, had had ten children by a first wife. After his first wife died, Cochran had married a widow, Mary Jane Cummings. Michael and Mary Jane already had two sons—five-year-old Albert and three-year-old Charles—when Elizabeth was born.

Mary Jane usually dressed Elizabeth in pink dresses and white stockings. Elizabeth stood out, since girls usually wore dark colors: gray or brown dresses and black stockings. Perhaps Mary Jane thought pink set off Elizabeth's hazel eyes. Or perhaps, as one historian has speculated, Mary Jane wanted her daughter "to attract attention and revel in it." Elizabeth (who, as she grew up, secretly wished her stockings were black) was called "Pink" or "Pinkey."

Pink's father was a model member of his community. Michael Cochran's father had died when the boy was only four. Michael's mother had apprenticed him to learn the blacksmith trade. By the time Michael was a young man of nineteen, he was running his own blacksmith shop.

Michael Cochran was ambitious, and his shop prospered. He began investing his profits, buying land in Pitts' Mills, a tiny village near the larger town of Apollo, Pennsylvania. Over time, Cochran bought the mill, built a general store nearby, and moved his family into a comfortable two-story brick house.

In 1850, Cochran was elected to the post of associate county justice. He did not need a law degree to hold this post; many men who served as associate justices had no formal legal training. In 1855, at the end of Cochran's term, the county honored him by giving Pitts' Mills a new name, Cochran's Mills. After that, Cochran was known as the "Judge."

Little Pink chewed gum and loved horses. By the time she was five, she had a younger sister and brother, Catherine (Kate) and Harry. Pink adored them both. Pink played not only with her brothers and sister, but also with her nieces and nephews, who were children near her own age.

Cochran's Mills, meanwhile, was growing into a small town. The Judge's finances rapidly improved, and soon he was prosperous enough to buy a three-acre plot in nearby Apollo. He ordered a new house built there. Since Pink's half brothers and sisters were grown, only the Judge's second family moved into the new home.

The new house was built on a city street called Mansion Row because of the grand houses that lined it. The Cochrans' two-and-a-half-story home was no exception. It had 10,000 square feet filled with fine furniture. Pink loved exploring the house's library. She and her siblings roamed the acres surrounding the house, playing with the family's two dogs or visiting the family's cow and horse. Pink celebrated her sixth birthday that first happy year in Apollo.

Then Pink's world abruptly changed. Her father, struck suddenly with an illness that paralyzed him, died. As the family grieved, they learned that he had not made out a will. Mary Jane was no doubt stunned. In Pennsylvania in the 1870s, a husband alone owned his family's property. A wife could inherit his estate only if her husband's will designated her as his sole beneficiary.

Judge Cochran's son Robert, who was older than his stepmother, filed a petition asking that the Judge's estate be divided among all the heirs. In a decision that was undoubtedly heartbreaking for Mary Jane and her children, the state ruled that Cochran's property would have to be sold so that its value could be distributed. Pink's beautiful new house of a year would be auctioned.

The law did ensure that a widow receive no less than one-third of her husband's estate. This portion was called the "widow's third." Mary Jane's third was not enough, however, to enable her to buy her house at auction. It was bought by Colonel Samuel Jackson, the town's banker.

Each of the Judge's adult children received their shares of his estate outright. Mary Jane's inheritance and that of her five children, who were minors, would be held in trust. The children's trusts would be monitored by a court-appointed guardian, who turned out to be none other than Colonel Jackson, the new owner of Pink's former home.

Mary Jane's allowance from the trusts was modest, barely enough to meet the family's basic needs. And in the late nineteenth century, many careers open to men were closed to women. She could not easily get a job. Pink's family confronted the reality of a much reduced standard of living. They moved into an older, more modest home just a short distance from their former mansion. Furniture and children were crammed into the small space.

Despite the dramatic change in Mary Jane's circumstances, she made sure Pink learned how to play the piano and the organ. The skinny young girl still loved horses and horseback riding. On Sundays, the family attended the nearby Methodist Episcopal Church. The children went sledding in winter and rolled barrel hoops in summer. After a while, life did not seem so bad.

For Pink's mother, however, day-to-day life was difficult. She was a twice-widowed woman struggling to bring up five children on very little money. In January 1873, Mary Jane remarried. Her new husband was John Jackson Ford, a Civil War veteran who had become a widower not long before. Pink was eight years old.

The Cochran family was now the Ford family. Once again, life changed for Pink, Albert, Charles, Catherine, Harry, and their mother. The children's stepfather was often unemployed and so was of little help financially. Worse, he was a violent man, especially when he was drunk. "He is very cross," Pink said of him. Pink watched her mother cry when Ford called Mary Jane names. She saw Ford beat and choke Mary Jane.

Once Ford tracked the family to a New Year's Eve party and waved a pistol at Mary Jane. Another time, he started an argument at home. He dashed his coffee on the floor, threw a meat bone at Mary Jane, pulled out his gun, and lunged at his wife. Pink and Albert jumped into Ford's path, giving Mary Jane and the other children a chance to run out of the house. Pink and Albert quickly followed. Ford then nailed the doors and windows shut so that no one could return.

Divorce was rare and difficult in the 1800s. Divorced people, especially women, were considered failures and were often snubbed by others. In Armstrong County, Pennsylvania—where Pink and her family lived—only fifteen divorce actions were filed in 1878 out of a population of forty thousand. Only five of those actions were filed by women.

One of those women was Mary Jane. Her fear of Ford outweighed whatever stigma she might suffer by filing for divorce. She believed divorce was the only way to escape from the man who had thrown her family's life into such turmoil.

Sometimes, a court refused to grant a divorce. Mary Jane's neighbors, her children, and Mary Jane herself all testified at the court hearing to support Mary Jane's case. Albert testified that Ford had tried to murder Mary Jane. Pink, though just fourteen, also took the stand. "Mother was afraid of him," Pink told the court. Although Pink's name had become Elizabeth Ford, she would not use that name. She

Bly at twenty-six. Even at fourteen, she was spunky enough to testify in court on her mother's behalf.

signed the transcription of her testimony Pinkey E. J. Cochran. In June of 1879, Mary Jane was granted her divorce.

Pink now had to consider her future. Her options as a girl of definitely modest means in the 1870s were limited. Marriage within a few years was a possibility, but Pink's experience had taught her that marriage held no guarantees. And jobs for women were scarce. However, one profession—teaching—was a possibility.

Pink decided to attend the Indiana State Normal School at Indiana, Pennsylvania. The school was a vocational institution that trained both young men and women for teaching and business careers. Education there, however, was not cheap. To graduate from the three-year teacher's program, Pink would need more than four hundred dollars. Pink went to her financial guardian, Colonel Samuel Jackson, who assured her that she had enough money to complete the program.

Fifteen-year-old Pink enrolled in the fall of 1879. Her brothers Albert and Charles had recently left home and struck out on their own. Pink wrote to Charles telling him

Pink attended Indiana State Normal School for just one semester.

how excited she was about school and asking him to send money to their mother. She spent the fall engrossed in reading, writing, grammar, arithmetic, and drawing.

At school, Pink spelled her last name "Cochrane," adding an "e" to her father's surname. This spelling was the same as that of a prominent family in Apollo. Albert and Charles soon made the same change. Perhaps Mary Jane's three oldest children were reinventing themselves, reaching back to a time when they had belonged to a respectable family.

At the end of the fall semester, Pink headed home to Apollo. There she got a rude surprise. Despite what Colonel Jackson had told her, she found when she examined her account that she did not have enough money to return to school. Pink was bitterly certain that Jackson had lied to her and somehow mismanaged her trust, perhaps to his own benefit. With no other way to get school money, Pink was forced to drop out.

Pink had lost her father and then lived with a stepfather who was an abusive drunk. She had experienced the comfort of life with a good amount of money, only to see that snatched away. She had a mother who had needed Pink's protection, a mother straining to survive. And finally, Pink believed she had been betrayed by a financial guardian who should have been her advocate.

Again, the young woman had to consider her options. She could live at home in Apollo, with her mother. She could look for a husband. But Pink's losses had taken their toll. From now on, Pink would rely largely on herself. She had a third option, after all. She could find a new career.

Many poor working women and girls toiled in mills and factories in the late 1800s.

THREE

Pittsburgh

1880–1885

By early 1880, Pink's brothers Albert and Charles had found jobs in Pittsburgh, the nearest large city to Apollo. Located at the juncture of the Allegheny and Monongahela Rivers where the Ohio River begins, Pittsburgh was a noisy, thriving industrial center. Steel foundries and oil refineries fueled the city's economy. Jobs could be had at the city's many canneries and factories.

But while workers in Pittsburgh may have had jobs, their lives were gritty and impoverished. Wages were barely enough to cover necessities such as housing and food. Few workers had any money left over at the end of the month. Even children toiled away in the grimy factories, often because their families needed the extra money. Life was so grim that one late nineteenth-century writer said looking down on Pittsburgh from a nearby mountain was like "looking at hell with the lid off."

By the end of 1880, Mary Jane, along with Pink, Harry, and Catherine, joined Albert and Charles in Pittsburgh. The close-knit family at first lived in a small house in an industrial part of town. They later moved to a larger home where they could take in boarders to help make ends meet.

Men like Albert and Charles found employment easily in Pittsburgh. Heavy, physically demanding jobs were plentiful. Pittsburgh's thriving businessmen were also ready to hire men for white-collar positions such as clerk.

Women, if married, often stayed at home with their children. Those who needed to work could find jobs in Pittsburgh's factories. But white-collar jobs were hard for women to find. Pink's education, cut short as it had been, was of little help to her as she sought work as a nanny or tutor. For four years, she was one of many women unable to find steady and decent-paying employment.

Several daily newspapers flourished in Pittsburgh, including the *Pittsburg Dispatch* (the city's name was then spelled without an "h"). The *Dispatch* attracted readers with features such as its widely read column by Erasmus Wilson, who offered homespun wit and commentary on current topics. Wilson signed his columns with a pen name, "Quiet Observer," or sometimes simply "Q. O."

Pink read one of Wilson's columns, published in January 1885, in which Wilson responded to a letter he'd received from a reader calling himself "Anxious Father." Anxious Father complained that his five daughters, ages eighteen to twenty-six, were still living at home. "What am [I] to do with them?" Anxious Father asked Q. O. "Mother says to marry them off. I would do it in a minute if I had a chance, but they don't seem to catch on well."

In Wilson's reply, he chatted about the differences between boys and girls as they grew up. "In China and other of the old countries," Wilson wrote, "they kill girl babies or sell them as slaves, because they can make no good use of them. Who knows but this country may have to resort to this sometime—say a few thousand years hence." Wilson had failed to address the important question Anxious Father had asked. What was an unmarried girl, one who needed to provide for herself, to do?

Letters poured into the *Dispatch* office. "'Quiet Observer' is a fool—to put it mildly," wrote one reader. "I

The sky over Pittsburgh was often choked with smoke from its many industries.

used to like him real well, but since he got onto this woman question he is just as crazy as the rest of the men."

Another letter came from someone signing her name "Lonely Orphan Girl." Scrawled on a large sheet of paper, it stated that the writer was stymied in her attempts to find work simply because she was a woman.

Managing editor George Madden read the letter from Lonely Orphan Girl, then gave it to Wilson to glance over. "To have been judged by its appearance," Wilson later recalled, "it would have gone into the waste-basket, because there was no style about it." The two men chose not to print the letter. But somehow, it caught their attention anyway. Madden was "struck by the earnestness of the writer." She had passion. She wanted work, but could find none. Perhaps she might make a good reporter.

Madden determined to hire the young woman with the undeveloped journalistic talent he sensed. The problem was finding her. She had put no return address on her letter. Wilson suggested publishing an appeal in the *Dispatch* asking Lonely Orphan Girl to step forward. Madden worded the appeal this way: "If the writer of the communication signed 'Lonely Orphan Girl' will send her name and address to this office . . . she will confer a favor."

The next day, January 18, 1885, a young woman bounded into the paper's office asking where she could find the editor. Someone pointed out Madden. "She smiled for the first time," recalled Wilson, who was watching, "showing a beautiful set of teeth."

The girl with the beautiful smile was Lonely Orphan Girl, Pink Cochrane. Madden asked her his surprising question. Would Pink write an article for the *Dispatch?* Madden would personally edit it.

Few women worked as journalists in the 1880s. Those who did mostly wrote "puff pieces," feature articles about weddings and other social events. Rarely did women reporters cover breaking news stories or serious political issues.

For many Americans, especially American women, the political and economic status of women was becoming a serious political issue. Pink's article for the *Dispatch,* published on January 25, 1885, and entitled "The Girl Puzzle," addressed the question Wilson had dismissed. She wrote, "The anxious father still wants to know what to do with his five daughters. They cannot marry or will not as the case may be, all marry. . . ."

Pink pointed out the difficulties for women trying to find jobs, particularly jobs that would provide a decent living. She lamented the fact that men easily found work that paid well enough, while women, if they were lucky enough to find a job, were placed in menial, low-paying positions.

"If girls were boys quickly would it be said: start them where they will, they can, if ambitious, win a name and fortune, . . ." Pink wrote. "Let a youth start as an errand boy and he will work his way up until he is one of the firm. Girls are just as smart, a great deal quicker to learn; why, then, can they not do the same?"

"The Girl Puzzle," before editing, was "pretty 'rocky' as far as grammar was concerned," according to Wilson. But it had the foundation of solid reportage. As Wilson—who admired rather than resented Pink's response—put it, "It contained all the facts."

Young as she was, Pink wove the passion of her own experience into her article. She observed that many young girls and boys were working but still poor, calling them "poor little ones put in factories while yet not in their teens so they can assist a widowed mother, or perhaps father is a drunkard or

Erasmus Wilson was a well-known columnist for the Pittsburg Dispatch.

has run away," she wrote. Madden attached Pink's original pseudonym to the article, giving it the byline "Orphan Girl."

After publishing "The Girl Puzzle," Madden decided to hire Pink as a full-time reporter. Would she write for the *Dispatch's* new Sunday edition? Madden would pay her five dollars a week. Pink accepted. Quite unexpectedly, the Lonely Orphan Girl had gained entrance into an exclusive, largely male club.

While "Orphan Girl" had been an appropriate byline for "The Girl Puzzle," Madden wanted a different pen name for his new reporter, "something neat and catchy," as Wilson recalled. Staff members made several suggestions; one shouted out, "Nelly Bly." The name came from a song by popular songwriter Stephen Foster, who was from Pittsburgh. Madden liked the name, and the debate was over. Rushing to make the next edition's deadline, Madden quickly affixed the name "Nellie Bly" to Pink's article. He had spelled the name differently from Foster's song. No matter. Pink Cochrane was known to her readers as Nellie Bly from then on.

In Bly's first work as a staff reporter, she undertook a series of articles on the experiences of Pittsburgh's poor working girls and women. Bly chose an unusual approach, one that didn't focus on the obvious—women's lives at work.

The "Nelly Bly" in Stephen Foster's popular song was an African-American servant girl.

Instead, Bly went after the stories of individual women's experiences when the workday was over.

One woman factory worker told Bly, "I work hard all day, week after week, for a mere pittance. I go home at night tired of labor and longing for something new, anything good or bad to break the monotony of my existence. I have no pleasure, no books to read. I cannot go to places for want of clothes and money, and no one cares what becomes of me."

Bly included many such comments in her series, which ran for two months in the *Dispatch's* Sunday edition. Bly added stories about working conditions inside factories. She touched on the use of child laborers, which many reform-minded people of the 1880s believed to be wrong.

Bly's spelling and grammar were still "pretty rocky." But Madden and Wilson could fix those problems. Bly brought something fresh to her work. Her penchant for focusing on the individual within a larger story gave her articles a vivid immediacy.

Abruptly, after this series, Madden gave Bly a new assignment. Like most women working for daily newspapers, Bly was to cover "women's" interests such as gardening, fashion, and society happenings. Such stories were usually gathered together in a section called the "women's pages."

While Bly certainly had steady work, she did not really have a reporting challenge. She quickly grew frustrated with her place in an insignificant part of the newspaper. She pleaded with Madden to let her write a weekly column instead. Madden agreed. Bly could cover any topics she found inter-esting—her take on anything happening in Pittsburgh that might affect her readers.

Given the chance to choose her own topics, Bly again fo-cused on the plight of the city's poor working girls. In her column, she offered suggestions for improving their lives. One suggestion was to establish a place where girls could gather after work. This place could be a sanctuary similar, Bly said, to one available to young men through the Young Men's Christian Association (YMCA), which offered a reading room as well as a bed for the night to young men needing a temporary place to stay.

Bly put much of her own personality and actions into her stories. Readers approved. "If we had more people like Bly to think of something for the good of the working girls," wrote one, "it would be better for us." Bly also received encouragement from Erasmus Wilson, who was fast becoming her mentor.

Even so, Madden moved Bly back again to the women's pages. His reasons are not known, although he may have been pressured by advertisers to reign her in. Again, Bly would cover topics such as hair care, tree grafts, and the new fashion of rubber raincoats. These were of little interest to Bly. At twenty-one, she had been a newspaper writer for just nine months. Even so, she already expected better assignments. "I was too impatient to work along at the usual duties assigned women in newspapers," she said later.

At the end of 1885, as Pittsburgh lay covered in snow, Bly resigned. She had "conceived the idea of going away as a correspondent." If Madden would not let her dig for interesting news in Pittsburgh, she would find it elsewhere. Madden agreed to publish articles she would write as a freelancer. So away she went—to sun-drenched Mexico.

NELLIE IN MEXICO.

She Finds a Great Many Odd Things to Write About.

THE FATE OF FEMALE CORRESPONDENTS.

Scanty Dress the Prevailing Style in the Country and Small Towns.

MARRYING INTO PERPETUAL SLAVERY

Special Correspondence of the Dispatch.

CITY OF MEXICO, February 12.—Journalists from the States are not regarded with much favor by the people of Mexico. So many have come here who were unable to speak the language, and so careless of truth, that they misrepresented everything.

Even now Mexicans are laughing about a lady who came here to represent some New York magazines. Renting rooms out from the city, she retired with books on Mexico she had obtained at different stores, and without making an observation or seeking to know the truth, she wrote from the books and sent the articles back to the States. A railroad conductor found much amusement in coaching her. Once, on being pressed by her to tell something of the people, he said that they roasted whole hogs, heads and all, without cleaning, and served them on the table. She jotted the story down as a rare item. Although her stay was very short, and she saw nothing of Mexican life, not having been been admitted into any families, she is still contributing articles on Mexico the Eastern press.

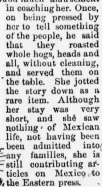

A Native.

Male writers are as much at fault as the women, but at the present day there are no less than six widows, of the crankest type, writing up Mexico, each expecting to become a second Humbolt and have their statues erected on the public square.

There are numerous men here representing papers, but I cannot speak of their ability. One thing is sure, they have only the old

night, they can be seen pursuing their different occupations with a real Pittsburg vim. For the matter of a few cents difference with the railroad on freight, they will load up a train of burros with fruit, hay, clover or earthenware, and travel for days until they

The Plow in Use.

reach the city. The burros are hitched up in no way, and trot along obediently to the call of their masters, the Mexicans.

TOMATOES AND STRAWBERRIES.

While yet a day's travel distant from the City of Mexico, tomatoes and strawberries were procurable. The venders are quite up to the tricks of the hucksters in the States. In a small basket they place cabbage leaves and two or three small pebbles to give weight; then the top is covered with strawberries so deftly that even the smartest purchaser thinks he is getting a bargain for 25 cents.

Wheat and barley are never cut by machines, but pulled up by the roots. Haystacks, although the shape of ours, are built with the point, or top, on the ground, just exactly like ours if they were turned upside down. When the people turn out to a husking bee, they do not return to their homes so long as there is any work to be done. They build fires with the husks and sleep on the ground.

Men owning large farms build very substantial homes for their people, and every farm has its church and priest. One of the curses of the poor is marriage. They will not be married by a Justice of the Peace, because it permits of divorce, and their priests have, in many instances, asked so much as $200 for a single marriage. Then the poor fellow, who is determined to marry, goes to a farmer and sells himself and wife for the marriage fee. They know their fate. During

---

The headline for one of Bly's articles advertised "Nellie in Mexico." Bly always seemed to see her name in print—an unusual distinction.

FOUR

Mexico

1886–1887

On a cold night in February 1886, Bly and her mother said good-bye to a few friends and climbed aboard a train headed south. Bly intended to send Madden a series of articles about Mexican life.

Mexico at that time was led by President Porfirio Díaz. Díaz presented his country to the outside world as a democracy. But in fact, Díaz ruled Mexico with the iron grip of a dictator. A corrupt man, Díaz encouraged foreign investment in Mexico, supposedly to benefit its many poor peasants. Instead, he looted much of the wealth for himself and his powerful military and business allies.

There were many newspapers in Mexico, but their editors made sure articles never criticized Díaz or his government. If a newspaper published criticism, it might be shut down and the writer of the unfavorable story jailed. Foreign correspondents such as Bly worked under the threat of imprisonment just as much as Mexican journalists did. For this reason, readers in the United States had little knowledge of the true nature of the political situation in Mexico.

In addition, United States citizens had little knowledge of the Mexican people. Many people in the United States held a sweeping stereotype that Mexican people were lazy, ignorant, and unclean.

Bly wanted to see for herself what life in Mexico was really like. Her mother had joined her as chaperone. In the 1880s, proper young women did not travel alone. At one point, Bly and Mary Jane were the only two women aboard their train.

Three days after leaving Pittsburgh, Bly and Mary Jane woke to warm sunshine. Their train had crossed into Texas. The passing countryside looked nothing like Pennsylvania. "We gazed in wonder at the groves of cacti which raised their heads many feet in the air, and topped them off with one of the most exquisite blossoms I have ever seen," Bly later told her readers. Less pleased, Bly also observed "women plow-ing while their lords and masters sat on a fence smoking." Even though Bly was whisking by on a train, she managed to put herself into the setting. "I never longed for anything so much as I did to shove those lazy fellows off," she wrote.

The next day, the two arrived in the City of Mexico (as Mexico City was then called) and settled into a hotel. Bly be-gan to write almost immediately. She wanted, first, to explain her mission to her readers. "In Mexico, as in all other coun-tries, the average tourist rushes to the cathedrals and places of historic note, wholly unmindful of the most intensely in-teresting feature the country contains—the people."

Bly quickly decided she could not tell readers much about Mexico's "most intensely interesting feature" by staying in a hotel. She made arrangements for her mother and herself to stay with a Mexican family. Then she set out to explore.

Bly sent back a flurry of dispatches to Madden that gave readers a feeling that they were in Mexico with her. She commented on the way the streets were named, on new construction in the city, and on the number of babies Mexican women seemed to have. Missing no detail, she listed the ways Mexican cemeteries differed from those found in the United States, mused about the Mexican people's love of cigarettes, and gossiped about the doings of celebrity visitors to the city.

Much of what she wrote seemed to contradict stereotypes. "The Mexicans are certainly misrepresented, most wrongfully so," she told her readers back in Pittsburgh. "They are not lazy, but just the opposite. From early dawn until late at night they can be seen filling their different occupations." Mexican people had other good qualities, too. "As a people they do not seem malicious, quarrelsome, unkind or evil-disposed," she wrote. "Drunkenness does not seem to be frequent, and the men, in their uncouth way, are more thoughtful of the women than many who belong to a higher class."

The hardships of the poor peasant people tugged at Bly just as the hardships of Pittsburgh's working girls had. "Their condition is most touching," she wrote. "Homeless, poor, uncared for, untaught, they live and die. They are worse off by thousands of times than were the slaves of the United States. Their lives are hopeless, and they know it."

At one point, Bly noticed a merchant trying to cheat a poor Indian man by giving him change in counterfeit money. She made herself a central character in the drama as she told it. "My American love for justice was aroused," she wrote. "And in broken English and bad Spanish I managed to tell him I knew the money was bad, and that the merchant was like the money."

Even the recipes she shared showed a new side of Mexico. "Probably some one would like to make a few of the dishes most common to the Mexican table," she wrote in an article

Bly gave her readers a sense of the contrast between Mexico's rich and poor.

explaining how tortillas were made. "Of course you will think them horrible at first, but once you acquire the taste, American food is insipid in comparison."

Bly had intended to stay in Mexico for at least six months. But five months into her adventure, she faced the Mexican government's censorship. A Mexican editor had recently been arrested for writing editorials against the government. Bly reported the story in the *Dispatch*. When Mexican authorities learned of her article, they became angry at the bad light in which it portrayed them. Government agents confronted Bly and threatened to arrest her.

"I did a good deal of what is commonly called 'bluffing' in regard to the power of the American government to protect the freedom of her citizens and the press," she said. The bluffing worked; Bly was not thrown into jail. Still, she decided, it was probably time to leave Mexico.

Bly and her mother returned to Pittsburgh in July. Safe now from Díaz, Bly continued her Mexican articles for the *Dispatch* in a more critical tone. In one, she called the Díaz government "the worst monarchy in existence."

Within a few months, Bly rejoined the *Dispatch* as a full-time, staff reporter. Perhaps she presumed she'd earned better assignments than garden parties. Madden obliged, in a way. He gave Bly a beat that he may have considered to be a reward—covering the theater and other arts.

Bly was disappointed. "It was too dull" for her, Erasmus Wilson recalled. "The city editor couldn't find anything to her taste, and they jarred and fussed a good deal."

One day, three months after Bly had returned to the *Dispatch,* she did not show up for work. According to Wilson, who by now had become Bly's friend as well as her mentor, no one had any idea where she was. Then Wilson found a note. It read: "Dear Q. O. I am off for New York. Look out for me. Bly."

New York City's Park Row was lined with the offices of some of the nation's most prestigious newspapers. City Hall can be seen at the far left.

FIVE

The "Mysterious Waif"

1887–1888

Bly arrived in May 1887 in the largest, wealthiest, and most congested city in the nation. The Brooklyn Bridge, a great engineering achievement, had recently been constructed over the East River; scores of horse-drawn carriages traveled across the bridge each day. Italian and Eastern European immigrants, newly arrived in the city, had set up shops throughout the Lower East Side. The sounds of dozens of different languages filled the air.

Bly was keenly aware that New York City was the center of newspaper publishing in the United States. Other large cities, such as Chicago, Boston, and St. Louis, had well-established newspapers. But it was the New York papers that carried the most national influence. The self-confident Bly, with her reporting background, probably expected to be quickly hired by one of them.

Bly's mother had traveled with her. From a small furnished room they rented on the city's Upper West Side, Bly made the rounds of all the daily newspapers, especially the powerful papers whose offices stood along New York City's famous Park Row—the *New York Times, New York Herald, New York Tribune,* and *New York World.* But for several months, Bly could not even get past the security guards at their doors.

Unfortunately for Bly, two obstacles stood between her and her goal. The first was the intense competition among many reporters who, like her, wanted to sign on with the country's largest newspapers. The second problem was familiar: The newspaper world was largely a man's world. Park Row was certainly not a genteel environment. Male reporters swore and smoked cigarettes. One of the highest ranking editors, John Cockerill of the city's most powerful newspaper, the *New York World,* had once shot and killed a man in self-defense.

But Bly had made it into the journalism club before and was determined to do it again. With the savings that was supporting both her mother and herself rapidly running low, Bly needed to turn this difficult situation to her own advantage. Most reporters and editors were male; perhaps Bly could use that fact to promote herself. Bly decided to interview New York's top editors for a freelance story she would write for the *Pittsburg Dispatch.*

Bly contacted every top editor in the city and quickly got her interviews. Her story, she explained, would answer the question: Is New York City the best place for a woman to get started in journalism? The editors were only too happy to give advice. And for the most part, their advice was that a woman should steer clear of newspaper work. At the *New York Herald,* editor George H. Hepworth explained that "a gentleman could not in delicacy ask a woman" to report scandals such as police and courtroom news. John Cockerill told Bly that, as a reporter, "a man is of far greater service."

Bly wrote her story for the *Dispatch,* and it was reprinted in two New York papers. But she was no closer to getting the reporting job she coveted.

The owner and publisher of the *New York World* was Joseph Pulitzer, who had purchased the paper four years earlier. In that short time, Pulitzer had made a number of changes that catapulted the *World* to the forefront of late nineteenth-century journalism. An immigrant himself, Pulitzer had tailored the paper to the masses of immigrants and working-class people with which New York City was over-flowing, waging hard-hitting editorial campaigns for causes to benefit them. Clearly, the strategy worked. The circulation of the *World's* Sunday edition alone climbed from 20,000 to 200,000 under Pulitzer's leadership.

A significant feature of what later became known as "New Journalism" was a Pulitzer innovation called "stunt reporting." Stunt reporting was an early form of investigative journalism. Investigative reporters working more than a century after Bly

In the nineteenth century, most newspaper jobs were held by men.

spend long hours following leads and talking to knowledge-able people to get their stories. A stunt reporter of the late 1880s, however, could skip that tedious groundwork. In one kind of stunt, the reporter concealed his identity as a reporter. Using a fake identity, he could quickly trick people into revealing things they would not have revealed to a reporter.

While unethical by later standards, this way of gaining in-formation was acceptable in Bly's time. Stunt journalists could expose corruption and bring injustice to people's attention. Their stories were popular. As readers clamored for more, cir-culation at the *World* increased and money poured in.

In September 1887, Bly hit a new low. She lost her purse. It had held most of the few dollars she had left. Bly was des-perate. She decided her best chance to get a newspaper job was to propose a stunt. Marching up to a security guard at the *World's* front door, she told him she had an important story. If he didn't let her in, she would go elsewhere with it. Once again, bluffing worked. Bly shortly found herself back in the office of John Cockerill. Eagerly, Bly ran a number of story ideas past him.

Cockerill was no doubt intrigued by the smartly dressed, fresh-faced young woman before him. But before making any offer to a reporter who was young, relatively inexperienced, and female, Cockerill knew he had to speak with Pulitzer. Cockerill gave Bly twenty-five dollars to keep her from going to another newspaper. Then he told her he would get back to her shortly.

In the months when Bly had been seeking work, several New York newspapers had featured articles about alleged abuses at a home for the insane on Blackwell's Island in the East River. Quoting some former patients, the articles said patients often had to eat spoiled food, live in filthy conditions,

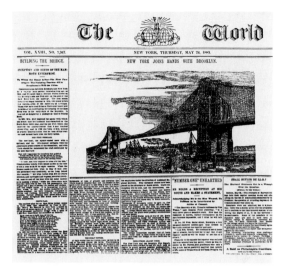

On May 24, 1883, the World reported the completion of the Brooklyn Bridge.

and endure beatings. Reporters could not verify the allegations, however. One reporter for *Harper's Weekly* was taken on a supervised tour of the asylum and found conditions to be quite tolerable. The ex-inmates making the allegations had once been insane, so their stories were suspect.

A stunt reporter, posing as an insane person, could gain admittance to the women's asylum and learn firsthand the truth about life for its inmates. No one knows whether it was Pulitzer or Cockerill who thought of hiring Bly to get into the asylum. But by the time the two had finished their meeting, Pulitzer had given Cockerill permission to let her try.

Cockerill called Bly back to his office and explained the assignment. Bly knew that if she succeeded in getting committed to the asylum, she might be thrust into danger. There were the allegations of beatings. Even worse, what if she were simply locked up and forgotten about? Cockerill promised he would find a way to get her out of the asylum. He would not abandon her.

Cockerill also explained that he was not offering Bly a permanent job; he was only trying her out to see how well she would do. He was asking a lot of Bly with little assurance of reward. But for Bly, the assignment was the break she needed. She may have sensed, too, that the story might generate great excitement if she succeeded in getting it. She eagerly accepted, and the *World* had its first stunt girl.

To prepare for her escapade, Bly went to the district attorney's office. Could she be prosecuted for the ruse? Assistant District Attorney Henry D. Macdona cautioned her against the danger. But when Bly jumped up, stomped her foot, and said nothing would scare her off, Macdona agreed to give her immunity.

Bly would have to become an actress if she were to fake her way into an asylum for the insane. As her next step, she "remembered all I had read of the doings of crazy people," she said. She practiced contorting her face and staggering around in a pretend daze. She stopped bathing. She would tell people her name was Nellie Brown, as Cockerill had instructed her, so that, if she were admitted to the asylum, the laundry markings on her clothes would match the pseudonym's initials.

After a few days, "Nellie Brown" was ready to emerge. Bly checked into a boardinghouse for women and immediately began acting the part of a deranged person. She muttered to herself and stared blankly at the other boarders. Her gibberish and stares worked to such great effect that one of her fellow guests was "afraid to stay with such a crazy being in the house."

While everyone else was uncomfortable, Bly was thrilled by the effectiveness of her disguise. She sat up all night, feeling that the "turned-down pages of my life were turned up."

The next day, the landlady called the police. Questioning Bly, they found she would not or could not divulge any clues to her identity. They took Bly to a courtroom, where, after a short wait, Bly faced Judge Patrick Duffy. Duffy asked Bly about her strange behavior. Her answers convinced him that Bly needed further examination. He ordered her taken to New York's Bellevue Hospital for psychiatric observation.

Duffy also decided to help the disoriented woman find her family. "Poor child," he said. "She is well dressed, and a lady. . . . I would stake everything on her being a good girl." Since Bly could not say whether she had any relatives, Duffy contacted various city reporters, hoping they would give Bly's case publicity that might lead to information about who she was and where she was from. "I am positive," he told them, "she is somebody's darling."

Four of New York's largest papers obliged, running features describing Nellie Brown and asking for help in finding her relatives. The *New York Times,* reporting on the "mysterious waif," said, "Her face was almost haggard in its paleness, and there was a wild, hunted look in her eyes." Meanwhile, the *World* published nothing. Its editors were having a good laugh about the free publicity their competition was generating.

After a battery of tests, examining doctors at Bellevue Hospital ruled out physical causes for Bly's strange behavior. They concluded that she was insane. The doctors could do little but order Bly taken to the dreaded Blackwell's Island.

On September 27, 1887, Bly was led with other new patients to a wharf in New York City's harbor. The new asylum inmates traveled to the island on a crowded ferry. Bly found the ferry's cabins oppressive, heavy with stifling air. At one end of Bly's cabin, a sleeping bunk was so filthy that Bly had to "hold [her] nose" when she went near it.

Ahead of Bly on the island, the imposing asylum buildings were grand, almost beautiful. But an oppressive air hung over the people inside. Bly carefully noted everything that went on as several days slipped by. She was forced to sit for hours without talking, reading, or doing anything that might relieve the boredom.

Daily life held many indignities. To bathe, Bly was led naked by female attendants to a tub. She stood, forlorn and shivering, as they threw buckets of ice cold water on her. With water in her mouth and ears and eyes, the gasping Bly felt as though she was drowning. "For once," she wrote when

Until Bly gained admittance to the asylum on Blackwell's Island, no one on the outside really knew what life was like for inmates.

she later described the scene, "I did look insane." Perhaps worst of all, Bly witnessed the physical abuse she had heard of; she saw attendants choke and push and slap patients.

Bly also observed her fellow inmates. She began to believe that some of them were not insane but merely immigrant women who spoke little or no English. These women had been declared insane, Bly believed, because they could not make anyone understand them. The asylum did not seem to be a hospital at all, but rather a prison for locking away unwanted and misunderstood people. Bly began to feel that the inmates, including herself, were caught in a "human rat-trap."

Meanwhile, the New York papers were still publishing requests for information about Nellie Brown. One day, a reporter showed up at the asylum. He said he was looking for a lost friend. In reality, he was trying to get a glimpse of Miss Brown. He soon found her. Unfortunately for Bly, the reporter was someone she knew, a man who at one time had worked at the *Pittsburg Dispatch,* Bly's old paper.

George McCain recognized Bly immediately. "I saw by the sudden blanching of his face and his inability to speak that the sight of me was wholly unexpected and had shocked him terribly," Bly said. Anxious to stop McCain from telling his readers who she really was, Bly begged him not to give her secret away. He agreed.

Ten days after Bly had been ferried to Blackwell's Island, an attorney from the *World* arrived. He had come to gain Bly's release. When he said he had found friends to care for Nellie Brown, the asylum released Bly. She was free.

As Bly headed out the door, she passed fellow inmates who were still imprisoned. "Sadly I said farewell to all I knew as I passed them on my way to freedom and life, while they were left behind to a fate worse than death," she wrote later.

The *World's* competitors were not amused when they learned of Bly's stunt. Although they had been giving the plight of Nellie Brown ongoing publicity, most ignored the way her story ended. But the *New York Evening Sun* complimented Bly. That paper said she was "too sharp for the island doctors" and called her "intelligent, capable, and self-reliant." Best of all, the *Sun* said Bly had "gone about the business of maintaining herself in journalism in a practical, businesslike way."

On October 9, 1887, the first of two installments of Bly's story was splashed across five columns of the *World's* front page. Bly's eyewitness account of abuses was published under the headline "Behind Asylum Bars." Bly revealed details about the harsh baths and sometimes rancid food. She told of beatings and of inadequate doctor's examinations that left sane women imprisoned. Word of Bly's shocking exposé traveled, and people snapped up copies of the newspaper as fast as they could be distributed.

Soon many people began to demand reform. The *World's* competitors followed public sentiment in condemning the treatment of Blackwell's Island patients. Newspapers throughout the United States featured editorials agreeing with them.

A grand jury was convened to look into the situation on Blackwell's Island. To help the asylum improve its conditions, jury members recommended increased funding for it. New York City's mayor, Abram Hewitt, acted quickly on the recommendation, providing one million dollars for improvements—money Bly referred to as the "one consolation for my work." Just as importantly, abusive nurses and attendants were removed. Icy baths and rotten food were eliminated.

Bly had both impressed and shocked her colleagues with the ability of a brand-new reporter to get such an important story. One respected reporter called her "bright as a new pin."

Even better, the *World* hired her as a full-time reporter. Bly also wrote a book called *Ten Days in a Mad-House.* She was invited to speak at meetings and fund-raisers throughout New York.

Bly's appearances generated a great deal of publicity as well as some pretty good money for her. Her name became well known throughout the country. And with her income from the lectures and her new reporter's salary, she was able to move with her mother out of their rented room and into a larger West Side apartment.

After the Blackwell's Island articles, Bly almost immediately wrote two more exposés. One revealed how newborn babies were sold to desperate couples in illegal adoption schemes. The other examined how employment agencies cheated applicants for domestic work. In each case, Bly assumed a fictional identity to get her story. She pretended to be an unwed mother for the adoption article and a maid for the employment agency story.

Bly had become a household name in the United States. But as impressive as Bly's entrance into journalism had been, it was overshadowed before long. Another, much bigger story by the mysterious waif was taking shape.

In 1890, Joseph Pulitzer built a new building for the World *just across from City Hall on Park Row.*

SIX

What Gave Me the Idea?

1888–1889

W hat gave me the idea?"

Many people try to avoid being associated with a bad idea. If a good one comes along, however, there is barely enough credit to go around. When Bly was asked who gave her the idea that made her internationally famous, Bly—who never shied from self-promotion—did not hesitate to claim it as her own.

In 1873, a French science fiction writer named Jules Verne published a novel entitled *Around the World in Eighty Days.* Hugely successful with readers, the book chronicled the fictitious journey of Phileas Fogg, an adventurer who set out to circle the Earth on a bet. Fogg's accomplishment in traveling nearly twenty-two thousand miles in a mere eighty days greatly intrigued readers. That speed was remarkable in a time when people plodded along in horse-drawn wagons and carriages. They crossed the ocean by sailing for days or weeks on ships.

Bly had been working hard for the *World.* Although just twenty-four, she'd masterminded dozens of exposés. One shocking story was her exposé of a powerful New York lob-byist, Edward R. Phelps. Bly helped to prove that Phelps was guilty of bribery and other illegal tactics in influencing the state assembly.

Bly stood out among reporters, male or female. She defied stereotypes about women. Perhaps for that reason, Belva Lockwood, a well-known lawyer, asked Bly to join the Women's Suffrage Party. The party was trying to gain women's right to vote in national elections. Bly said she couldn't join because reporters had to appear impartial. "I can help your movement more by putting into practice what you've been preaching," Bly told Lockwood.

Although some of Bly's stories were assigned, she was ex-pected, like other reporters, to suggest stories that would grab readers' attention. Even the most talented reporters had to strain to produce exciting articles every day. Late one night, while lying awake trying to conjure up new ideas, Bly re-membered the book by Jules Verne that she had recently read.

"I wish I was at the other end of the earth!" she thought as she restlessly tossed in bed. "And why not? I need a vaca-tion; why not take a trip around the world? . . . If I could do it as quickly as Phileas Fogg did, I should go."

The next day, Bly went to the office of a steamship com-pany to look at its collection of timetables. No one had ever come close to matching Phileas Fogg's record time in "girdling the globe." Yet Jules Verne's novel showed that in-novations such as the new transcontinental railroad across North America had made the world a smaller place. After studying ship routes and schedules, Bly decided a real person could match the fictitious Fogg's pace—or beat it.

Then Bly headed to the *World*. "Have you any ideas?" John Cockerill asked her as she sat down by his desk. "One," she answered timidly, thinking her idea might be too extreme, "too wild and visionary," as she put it. "I want to go around the world!"

Cockerill, no stranger to wild ideas, told Bly he'd already been in meetings with other editorial managers in which they had discussed sending a reporter on just such a journey. What better stunt for publicity for the *World,* after all, than a trip around the world? But the managers had only considered sending a man. When Bly proposed herself to the newspaper's business manager, he put the objection bluntly. "No one but a man can do this," he told Bly.

"Very well," Bly replied angrily, her eyes flashing. "Start the man and I'll start the same day for some other newspaper and beat him." The slender Bly's forceful words made the point. The *World* managers assured Bly she could have the assignment—*if* they decided to proceed with an around-the-world adventure.

Sometimes, a good idea seems to occur to lots of people at once. During the following months, several other reporters proposed the same idea to the *World.* Finally, on Monday evening, November 11, 1889, Bly received a note ordering her to the *World's* office at once. Unsure why she was being called there in such a hurry, Bly said, "I spent all my time on the way . . . wondering what I was to be scolded for."

Instead of scolding Bly, Cockerill greeted her by looking up from his writing and simply asking, "Can you start around the world day after to-morrow?" Bly had waited for months for this question. She replied, "I can start this minute."

Bly now had to make many preparations in haste. Some people assumed she would find a chaperone to travel with, as she had during her stay in Mexico. But Bly decided to travel alone. She did not want anyone to slow her down. Instead of a chaperone, Bly would have a letter provided by the *World,* asking the captains of the ships Bly would sail on to keep an eye on her.

Some people were concerned about the safety of a young woman traveling so far by herself. Perhaps the innocent-looking Bly did not seem well prepared to deal with thugs. "Someone suggested that a revolver would be a good companion piece," Bly said. "But I had such a strong belief in the world's greeting me as I greeted it, that I refused to arm myself."

To travel abroad, Bly, like anyone else, needed a passport. But a permanent passport would take too long to get if Bly were to leave so soon. The *World* sent a staff member to Washington, D.C., to obtain a special temporary passport for Bly from James G. Blaine, the nation's secretary of state.

Bly certainly could not manage as much luggage as she would have taken with her if she had been going on a simple holiday. She didn't want to have to retrieve any bags from the storage compartment of a train or ship, since stopping for luggage might make her miss connections. She would take with her only what she could carry in one hand satchel.

This posed a problem. Women's clothes in the nineteenth century were much bulkier than clothes a century later. The fabric was heavier, the skirts longer. And women's fashions included many layers of clothes. Bly pared down to the essentials: two outfits, one for warm weather and one for cool climates. To top her outfits off, Bly purchased a double-peaked cap (one with a brim both in front and in back).

To cover expenses, the *World* provided Bly with two hundred pounds in Bank of England notes and British gold, currency that would be accepted almost anywhere. Bly also packed some U.S. paper money as a test to see in which countries it would be accepted.

Unlike many women of her era, Bly was more than willing to travel light.

The last problem Bly needed to resolve before leaving was her itinerary. The *World* staff had been hurriedly trying to figure one out for her. Bly would travel eastward by ship and train, to Europe, the Middle East, Asia, and onward to North America. Bly's journey would end in Jersey City, New Jersey, just across the Hudson River from New York City.

While it was possible to buy tickets in New York for the entire trip, Bly decided the chance of having to change her travel plans as she went along was too great. She would leave the city with only a ticket for passage on a steamship bound for England.

Shot across the width of five columns of the *World's* November 14, 1889, edition was the story of Bly's challenge

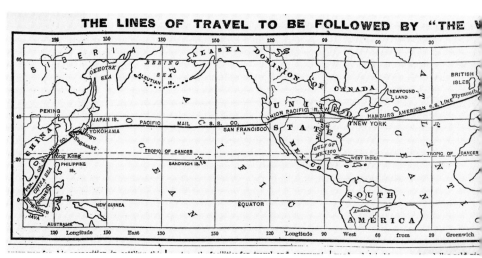

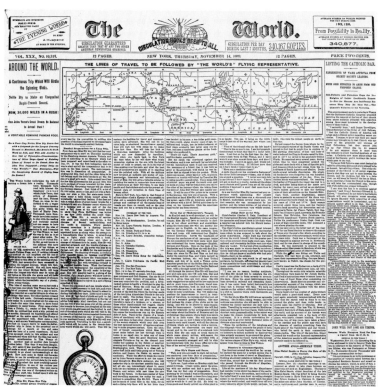

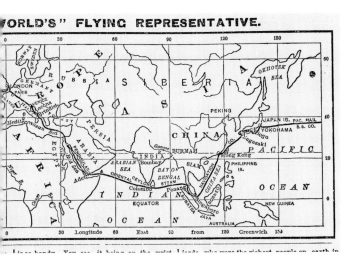

On November 14, 1889, the World *boasted: "Now 30,000 Miles in a Rush!" A map from the article, left, shows Bly's proposed route. The route actually covered about 22,000 miles.*

to turn Jules Verne's fantasy into fact. "A Continuous Trip Which Will Girdle the Spinning Globe" was the lead to the description of Bly's upcoming trip. Clearly, Pulitzer believed the trip would be a significant coup.

That same morning, Bly, along with a few friends, climbed aboard the steamship *Augusta Victoria.* The day was beautiful and clear, but when it came time for the friends to leave the ship, there were tearful farewells. "I tried to smile so that their last recollection of me would be one that would cheer them," Bly said.

At 9:40 A.M., the *Augusta Victoria* set sail, her propellers churning the water into a foamy wake. Bly "felt dizzy and my heart felt as if it would burst." As the liner pulled farther and farther out to sea, Bly gazed back at New York City. "I'm off," she said, thinking of the strangers and storms and unknown places ahead. "And shall I ever get back?"

Bly was twenty-five when she set out around the world. She laughed when women lied about their ages; but on her passport, she shaved two years off her own.

SEVEN

Twenty-Two Thousand Miles in a Rush

1889

Aboard the *Augusta Victoria,* passengers strolled the deck or climbed into reclining chairs, covering themselves with blankets to keep warm in the chill air. The ship swayed with each wave as it plowed ahead. While many of the passengers had taken sea voyages before, Bly never had. Nor had she ever encountered seasickness. The "demon of the sea," as Bly called it, appeared when someone asked Bly if she'd ever been seasick. "That was enough," Bly wrote. "I flew to the railing. I looked blindly down, caring little what the wild waves were saying, and gave vent to my feelings."

Afterward, she turned around to the smiles of passengers nearby. Their amusement didn't bother her, but the remark of one man did. He sneered, "And she's going around the world!"

As Bly's journey progressed, the weather took a turn for the worse. But Bly took a turn for the better. Even with rough seas pounding the ship, her seasickness was over. Bly turned her attention to the other passengers. She noted their habits

The Augusta Victoria *took Bly across the Atlantic Ocean.*

and traits—or rather, as Bly put it, their "peculiarities"—with the precision she'd shown in Mexico.

Back in New York City, the ink was barely dry on the *World's* announcement of Bly's departure when news came of a challenge. *Cosmopolitan* magazine had decided to sponsor one of its own reporters, Elizabeth Bisland, in a quest not only to beat Phileas Fogg's record, but also to beat Bly. Bisland would travel in the opposite direction around the world, on a westward route. The two reporters might even cross paths at some point.

The *Journalist,* a weekly magazine for editors and reporters, did not mention Bly and her sensational stunt. Editors at the *Journalist* considered themselves guardians of what they deemed to be the only "correct" kind of reporting: the kind listing only the dry facts. They didn't appreciate Pulitzer's methods in getting stories. Bly, as Pulitzer's stunt girl, was often a target of the *Journalist's* ire.

But about a week after Bly set sail, the *Journalist* did profile Bisland. The magazine praised Bisland as "a lady of the most charming manners, of the greatest refinement, as well as of considerable beauty." Best of all, Bisland was "in no sense a sensational writer."

Bly, however, was blissfully unaware. She received no telegraph cables aboard the *Augusta Victoria.* No newspapers linked her with the latest news; no trans-Atlantic telephone lines connected her with home. The news of Bisland's challenge would travel, but it would come along behind Bly.

A week after setting sail, the *Augusta Victoria* steamed into the port city of Southampton, England. Bly climbed aboard a tugboat that would ferry her to shore as many of the steamship's passengers gathered at the railing to wish her luck. Waiting for her on the tugboat was the *World's* London correspondent. He told Bly that Jules Verne had invited her to his home in Amiens, France. Without hesitation, Bly accepted the invitation.

But first Bly had to get to London. She had missed the last passenger train leaving for the British capital, but the train that would carry the *Augusta Victoria's* mail to London was about to depart. Railway officials, to accommodate the ship's passengers who'd missed connections, attached a passenger coach to the mail train, and the two journalists clambered aboard.

A heavy fog hung over London as Bly and her companion arrived in the city's Waterloo train station. They climbed into a horse-drawn cab and made a quick stop so Bly could pick up her permanent passport.

A frantic ride through the city's streets next brought the two to the Peninsular and Oriental Steamship Company. Bly's route would take her to Calais, France; Brindisi, Italy; Port Said, Egypt; Colombo, Ceylon; Singapore; Hong Kong; Yokohama, Japan; and San Francisco in the U.S.A. She bought tickets to cover about half the trip.

Then the two companions were off to Charing Cross train station. Famished, Bly downed a breakfast of ham, eggs, and coffee. Another dash took them to the English Channel and a waiting ferry. The air was bitterly cold as the ferry crossed the rough waters between England and France, but Bly stayed on deck, watching the seagulls and pondering her fate. She had heard a "stream of horrors" about ships lost in the crossing. As Bly looked down on the choppy water, "I naturally thought my time would come," she wrote.

But the two journalists safely reached the harbor of Boulogne, France. After a quick snack, they squeezed into the cramped passenger compartment of yet another train. This one would take Bly to Amiens, to Jules Verne.

Passengers board a train bound for Southampton, England, at Waterloo Station in London.

Waiting on the train platform in the French city were Verne, his wife, and a Paris journalist, R. H. Sherard. For the moment, Bly forgot she was a reporter and did what "any other woman would have done under the same circumstances," Bly said. "I wondered . . . if my hair was tossed."

Whether or not Bly was travel-stained and messy, Jules Verne's "bright eyes beamed" at her (as she later wrote) when they were introduced. The group climbed into two small carriages for the ride to the Vernes' home. Bly rode with Madame Verne. They spoke little, however; Bly could not speak French and her companion spoke no English.

Jules Verne also spoke no English, so, once the group was settled at the Vernes' home, Sherard translated. The talk naturally turned to Bly's journey. Verne asked Bly about her route. Bly could pronounce the names of the cities ahead of her without a translator. "I was very happy to speak one thing that he could understand," Bly thought as she ticked off her exotic itinerary.

The time came for Bly to end her visit with the author who had inspired her adventure. Bly could not miss the one train to Calais, France, or she might not be able to make up the lost time. In farewell, Verne spoke for the first time in English. "Good luck, Nellie Bly," he said. Then Bly was on her way.

As Bly had traveled, she had been writing articles on the fly. Some articles she cabled back to New York. Others went by ship. For that reason, her articles did not arrive day by day, one by one, as Bly wrote them. Instead, they arrived days apart and in bunches. Readers of the *World* might lose their interest in Bly's great adventure unless they were reminded of it daily. To keep the public hooked—and paying five cents a copy—the *World* invented a daily feature: a contest. Readers should guess the time of Bly's arrival back in New York.

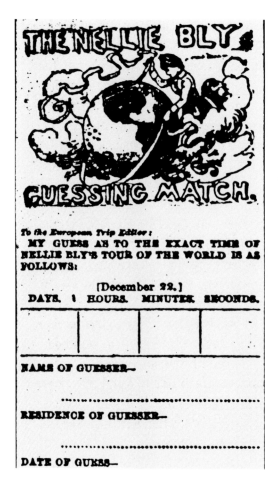

"The Nellie Bly Guessing Match" appeared every day in the World. *The person who came closest to guessing the exact time Bly would return to New York would win a trip to Europe.*

Whoever came closest would win a free trip to Europe. The *World's* contest kept circulation revenue flowing in. Dollars from advertisers poured in as well.

Meanwhile, Bly caught the train in Calais. As it passed into Italy, fog shrouded the tracks and slowed the train. Bly arrived in Brindisi, Italy, two hours late. Nonetheless, she made her connection with a British ship, the *Victoria,* which soon sailed for Port Said, Egypt.

Because a lady traveling so lightly was unusual, Bly caught people's eye. "I had not been on the Victoria many days until some one who had become friendly with me, told me it was rumored on board that I was an eccentric American heiress, traveling about with a hair brush and a bank book," Bly recalled. Some passengers took a more romantic view. Bly received two marriage proposals along the way.

After a brief stopover in Port Said, the *Victoria* continued ahead of schedule through the Suez Canal. The days were warm as the ship stopped at Ismailia, Egypt, and then steamed on to the Bay of Suez. As the *Victoria* floated at anchor, some fruit and souvenir merchants sailed out to hawk their wares. Bly helped readers see the scene along with her. She included descriptions such as that of a magician who arrived with the merchants.

The weather was very warm as the *Victoria* steamed on to Colombo, Ceylon, arriving on December 8, 1889—two days ahead of schedule. Bly was the first passenger ashore. She rushed to cable her editors at the *World* to tell them where she was. She was supposed to stay on the island of Ceylon for only a short time. But Bly soon learned that her next ship, the *Oriental,* could not leave Colombo for another five days.

The delay seemed like an eternity. Finally, Bly was aboard the *Oriental* and en route to Singapore. From there, the *Oriental* would sail on to Hong Kong, probably arriving soon enough that Bly could still make her next connection there.

Eight days later, the *Oriental* arrived outside Singapore after dark. The captain decided to anchor outside the city's harbor, intending to enter the busy port after daylight to lessen the chance of collision. Bly, contemplating the "precious hours" wasted, began to panic. "Those few hours might mean the loss of my ship in Hong Kong; they might mean days added to my record," she said. "What agony of suspense and impatience I suffered that night!"

The next morning, Bly and the other *Oriental* passengers arrived on shore in Singapore. Like any tourist, Bly explored shops and visited museums. She also took a rickshaw ride. The driver showed her the city and even took her to his home to meet his family—and their pet monkey. After many assurances that the monkey would not bite, Bly believed she rather liked it and bought it from the driver. Soon Bly and her unique souvenir were both aboard the *Oriental* and on their way to Hong Kong.

The ship made excellent progress. On the morning of December 23, the *Oriental* arrived in Hong Kong two days ahead of schedule. Weary of sightseeing, Bly's only desire in the exotic city was to get to the steamship office to purchase a ticket for the next leg of her journey. She had to leave as soon as possible for Yokohama, Japan, to win her race against time.

Rushing into the office of the Oriental and Occidental Steamship Company (the O. and O.), Bly asked when the line's next ship would sail for Yokohama. One of the employees invited her to sit down, which she did. He looked at her for a moment, then said, "You are going to be beaten."

"What? I think not. I have made up my delay," she tossed back, unless "the Pacific had sunk since my departure from New York."

"Aren't you having a race around the world?" the O. and O. man asked.

"Yes, quite right. I am running a race with time," Bly replied.

"Time? I don't think that's her name," was his answer.

"Her! Her!" Bly repeated.

"Yes, the other woman. . . . She left here three days ago,"

Hong Kong in the 1880s

the O. and O. man said. "I'm astonished you did not know any-thing about it. She led us to suppose that it was an arranged race."

Stunned, Bly for the first time learned of Bisland's chal-lenge. She tried to make sense of what she was hearing as the O. and O. employee explained the situation to her. She was now more eager than ever to push on, but she would have to stay in Hong Kong for five days. Since she would have to en-dure another five days in Yokohama, she might not make it back to New York in under eighty days. A person with better luck, as Bly knew from her study of timetables, could make the journey in as few as seventy.

"It's too bad," the O. and O. man said, "but I think you have lost it." Bly could do nothing. Resigned, she headed to her hotel and settled in to wait.

Canton, China. Bly visited Canton during her stopover in Hong Kong.

EIGHT

Alive and on Time

1889–1890

In the following days, Bly did some writing for the *World* and explored Hong Kong. She attended the theater, visited shops, and toured temples. On Christmas Eve, "after seeing everything of interest in Hong Kong," she traveled to the nearby Chinese city of Canton.

In what was certainly a strange scene for Christmas Day, the first place Bly elected to tour was the city's execution grounds. Sharing the horrors as well as the wonders of her trip with readers, Bly wrote, "A shiver waggled down my spinal cord." She also toured a leper colony and a temple.

Bly soon returned to Hong Kong. On December 28, she sailed east to Yokohama, Japan, aboard the *Oceanic*—the same ship Bisland had taken on her westward journey. On January 7, 1890, the *Oceanic* left Yokohama for the trip across the Pacific Ocean to the United States.

The *Oceanic* crew was well aware of Bly's challenger. They were happy to have a celebrity aboard and confident of Bly's success. The ship's chief engineer even had a couplet to her painted in the engine room:

For Nellie Bly,
We'll win or die.
—January 20, 1890

For the first two days of the voyage, the weather cooperated and the *Oceanic* made fast progress. But on the third day, the ship was hit by a massive storm. Rolling in heavy waves, the liner made slow progress. Bly despaired. "If I fail, I will never return to New York. I would rather go in dead and successful," she said, "than alive and behind time."

As the storm pounded the *Oceanic,* some passengers gave way to superstitious fears. They believed Bly's monkey was cursing the ship and suggested throwing the animal into the ocean. "A little struggle between superstition and a feeling of justice for the monkey followed," Bly said. Someone mentioned that ministers also brought bad weather to ships, and there were two aboard. Bly considered this. "So I said quietly, if the ministers were thrown overboard, I'd say nothing about the monkey." The monkey's life was spared.

Finally, the *Oceanic* passed through the storm. On January 20, the California coastline and the city of San Francisco appeared on the horizon. Bly was ecstatic. Suddenly the ship's purser, his face snow-white, rushed by her, crying out, "My God, the bill of health was left behind in Yokohama." The document was needed to vouch for the good health of the passengers. Without it, no one could land. The captain could telegraph to Yokohama for the papers, but it would take two weeks for them to arrive aboard another ship.

"The thought of being held two weeks in sight of San Francisco, in sight of New York almost, and the goal for which I had been striving and powerless to move, was maddening," Bly said. She told the purser she would simply cut her throat. Luckily, a second search turned up the missing papers.

Day after day of stormy weather slowed the progress of the Oceanic *across the Pacific.*

The next day, a tugboat pulled alongside the *Oceanic* to carry her passengers to shore. Bly and her monkey hopped aboard. At the dock, Bly stepped back on U.S. soil for the first time in nearly two months.

The shortest route east to Jersey City, New Jersey, was by railroad, over the Sierra Nevada. But a snowstorm had stopped all trains from crossing that mountainous terrain. This time, though, weather couldn't slow Bly down. Word of the storm had reached the *World,* and the paper had commissioned a special train for her. The train would take her south, around the storm, then east as far as Chicago. Within minutes of landing in San Francisco, Bly was aboard the train and setting off.

Public excitement over Bly's adventure was mushrooming. Throngs of well-wishers met her train at every stop. At first, the *World's* reporter scarcely realized the crowds of people had gathered to see her. When Bly saw a huge crowd at the train station in Merced, California, she "supposed they were having a picnic." Hearing her name called, she went out to the train's back platform. She was greeted by "a loud cheer, which almost frightened me to death."

Bly was surprised by the huge crowds that met her train.

Bly's train raced along the tracks at speeds of "over a mile a minute." At one point in New Mexico, workers tried to flag it down; the train was speeding toward a bridge that was under repair. But the train's engineer didn't see the warning in time. The train roared on. But nothing happened; Bly's train crossed safely. Her luck had held out.

By now, Bly knew Elizabeth Bisland had fallen behind. Although at one point Bisland had been ahead of Bly by almost three days, she, like Bly, had also missed connections. In addition, Bisland had counted on catching a very fast steamship, the *Etruria,* from Queenstown, England. Instead, a slow old ship, the *Bothnia,* had taken its place. As Bly drew closer and closer to New York, it seemed her victory was ensured.

The crowds continued to grow. At Topeka, Kansas, more than ten thousand people turned out to see Bly. At another stop, a band was prepared to perform for her. In the thrill of seeing the famous Nellie Bly, however, the musicians forgot to begin playing.

Bly's special train got her to Chicago in the fastest time on record. Thousands of miles of ocean and railroad line lay behind her. Now knowing that Bisland could not catch up with her, Bly would board a regular passenger train out of Chicago, and she had a little time before it was scheduled to depart. So members of the Chicago Press Club took her on a quick tour of the city.

One stop was the Chicago Board of Trade, where commodities such as grain and farm stock were being traded furiously. When Bly entered the enormous hall, trading was at its height. Brokers were furiously calling out their orders to buy and sell. Then someone shouted that Nellie Bly was there. The hall suddenly fell silent. "In one instant . . . every face, bright and eager, was turned up towards us . . . ," Bly

The mayor of Jersey City greeted Bly, as did many other well-wishers.

said. "Every hat came off, and then a burst of applause re-sounded through the immense hall." Calls came for Bly to speak, but she simply shook her head no and took off her trademark cap, drawing cheers.

Back at the train station, Bly was given a cable from Jules Verne and his wife. The cable had been sent to San Francisco but had missed her there. The Vernes offered their warm congratulations "to Miss Nellie Bly at the moment when that intrepid young lady sets foot on the soil of America."

Finally, Bly was once again on her way. In Philadelphia, hordes of reporters boarded her train to be with her on the last leg of her journey. Bly's mother also joined her globe-trotting daughter for this last part of the trip.

The Jersey City station was packed. As Bly's train pulled in, thousands of onlookers cheered; cannons thundered congratulations. It was 3:51 P.M. on Saturday, January 25, 1890. In seventy-two days, six hours, and eleven minutes, Bly had traveled 21,740 miles. She was back—"alive and on time."

Aboard the *Oceanic,* she had said, "If I fail, I will never return to New York." Now, within a carriage ride of her adopted city and with the proof of her triumph ringing in the applause all around her, she felt ecstatic. "I . . . wanted to yell with the crowd," she said, "not because I had gone around the world in seventy-two days, but because I was home again."

The difference in the sizes of these globes reflects the increase in the World's circulation under the leadership of Joseph Pulitzer. Bly's triumph added yet more readers and revenue to the paper.

NINE

Home

1890–1895

Bly certainly was home again—home to thousands of cheering fans. She was driven in a carriage to the *World's* New York City offices through streets jammed with onlookers. Everyone wanted a glimpse of her. The mayor of Jersey City credited Bly with changing the definition of American womanhood. "The American Girl will no longer be misunderstood," he said. "She will be recognized as pushing and determined, independent, able to take care of herself wherever she may go."

The *World* wasted no time in trumpeting Bly's success, running lengthy and numerous stories about her journey. According to one *World* article, Jules Verne was "in ecstasy over the achievement of 'The World's Voyager.'" Upon hearing of Bly's arrival in New York, according to the article, Verne had cried out, "Bravo! Bravo! Bravo!"

The *World's* competitors had to acknowledge Bly's feat. The *New York Times* ran an article admitting that "to all appearances she experienced no ill effect from her journey." John Brisben Walker, editor of *Cosmopolitan,* the magazine

"Around the World in 72 Days. Yes, We Always Get There!"
chortled this edition of Bly's paper.

that had sponsored Bisland's challenge, sent Bly a bouquet of
rare roses. Bly acknowledged the gift by saying the flowers
would "be treasured by the recipient among her most
thought-of tributes."

Bisland was still at sea. The *World's* editors gladly noted
that fact in a three-paragraph article with the headline "How
an Ambitious Young Woman Failed to Make a World Record."
Reported the article, "While Miss Bly was yesterday receiving the congratulations of her fellow workers in The World office, Miss Bisland, on the Bothnia, was wallowing in the
trough of the yeasty Atlantic." But the *World* could also afford
to be gracious, adding that Bisland "will have put a girdle
around the earth by the time she reaches New York, and she
will have added vastly to her cosmopolitan knowledge."

Cables of congratulations for Bly poured in from around the world. One came from the president of the Royal Geographical Society in England, Sir Mountetuart Grant Duff. Duff couldn't "see that her trip will benefit the cause of science, yet it shows what a plucky young woman with a powerful newspaper to back her can do." Bly was a "remarkable young woman," said Duff, and added his wishes for what he considered a woman's highest achievement. "I hope," he said, "she will get a good husband."

Not everyone was impressed with Bly's pluck. *Metropolis* magazine sniffed, "Nellie Bly has returned from her trip around the world. What of it?" Also critical, as usual, was the *Journalist's* Allan Forman. Bly's trip, wrote Forman, proved nothing but "the immense resources of the New York World . . . [and] that the great majority of the American people dearly love a sensation—no matter how flimsy—so long as it gives them something to gabble about." In fact, he argued, the *World* could just as easily "have sent a canvas-covered sugar-cured ham with a tag tied to it spinning around the globe."

Forman noted the tremendous jump in the *World's* circulation, which had increased by 24,000 copies since before Bly began her trip. Bly's adventure, Forman argued, "has shown that a young woman sent around the world for no practical purpose will work to greater advantage in booming a newspaper than a dozen men sent out after facts. It has been a great advertisement for the New York World and Miss Nellie Bly." In short, Forman concluded, "It paid."

But Forman's cynicism was not shared by most. Sold-out crowds gathered at speaking engagements arranged for Bly. A Nellie Bly game that retraced her route sold well. A cap, just like the one Bly wore on her trip, was offered for sale to young women. The *World* also published an "authentic biography" of Bly, revealing who she really was "in full." Nellie Bly had become "the most talked about woman in America."

Bly's pleasure at her success was short-lived. She expected that, for all the publicity and money her stunt had brought the *World,* she would be well compensated by the paper. Although Pulitzer had cabled his congratulations to his world-famous reporter, not a raise, a bonus, or barely a thank you from the newspaper were forthcoming, as Bly wrote to a colleague in a letter. The *Journalist,* hearing of the slights, wrote that her "ill treatment" by the *World* was "well known."

Bly had scrambled her way through frightening storms and weary nights and heartbreaking delays in her dash around the globe. She was the heroine for whom thousands of fans would "win or die." Yet she felt slighted by her own paper. The trip was over; Bly was home but with nothing solid to show for it. In disgust, she abruptly quit Pulitzer and the *World.*

Bly was living with her mother, her sister Kate, and Kate's daughter Beatrice in an uptown apartment. Now without a job, Bly, who was supporting the family, was intent on earning money. She quickly wrote a book chronicling her adventures. By the end of August 1890, *Nellie Bly's Book: Around the World in Seventy-Two Days* had sold more than ten thousand copies at fifty cents each.

Bly also signed a lucrative writing contract. She was to write fiction in serial installments for Norman L. Munro. The three-year contract with Munro's *New York Family Story Paper* would pay her ten thousand dollars the first year and fifteen thousand for each of the following years—phenomenal sums for the time. The generous contract was surprising because Bly's only experience in writing fiction had been a novel published in 1888, *The Mystery of Central Park.* That book had

Bly in 1896. Her job with the New York Family Story Paper *did not work out as planned.*

been a failure both with critics, who gave it bad reviews, and with the public, who simply did not buy it.

Bly quickly wrote to her old mentor at the *Pittsburg Dispatch,* Erasmus Wilson, with news of her deal with Munro. "I had made up my mind never to work for a newspaper again," she told him, but the serial stories were just what she needed. Perhaps Bly was disillusioned not only with newspapers but also with voyages; the best thing about the new arrangement, she told Wilson, was that she could do the serial work "and never go out of my own house."

No copies of Munro's *New York Family Story Paper* are known to survive, so it is unclear how many serial stories by Bly ever were published. But evidently, within a year of leaving the *World,* Bly had dropped out of sight. The *Journalist* ran an article asking, "Where is Nellie Bly? I don't mean the song, but the girl." In another issue, it questioned, "What is Miss Nellie Bly doing now?"

Bly wrote to Wilson expressing a sense of loneliness in her separation from the hustling world of journalism. She begged him to come to New York to visit her and her mother and Bly's menagerie, the well-traveled monkey and a dog and parrot she now owned. Wilson should travel east, she said, "before the monkey knocks the life out of the parrot and the dog shakes the impishness out of the monkey." As for herself, she confessed that she was becoming "a victim of the most frightful depression that can beset [a] mortal." In another letter, she said, "Strange to say, I have not the least conception of why I am, or should be, blue."

Allan Forman might have had an answer to that. In the view of articles published in the *Journalist,* Bly's accomplishments meant little. In fact, the *Journalist's* opinion of newspaper women was generally poor. "To be a power on the staff of a live, wide-a-wake, influential publication, requires brains . . . more than ordinary ability of rapid expression, and a strong sense of what is news," it said. Newspaper women didn't have those qualifications. They were "scribblers, writers, authors, anything but members of the press." As for Bly in particular, "literary merit had little to do" with her fame. "Her successes," according to the *Journalist,* "were only in the line of doing odd things."

Before long, Nellie Bly did another typically "odd thing." In the September 17, 1893, issue of the *World,* a headline at the top of a slim column announced the fact. It read "Nellie Bly Again." Whether scribbler, writer, author—or by any other name—Bly, just three years after leaving the *World,* was back on the beat.

She plunged right in. For her first story, she interviewed Emma Goldman, a well-known anarchist. Over the following months, she covered murders and politics and other significant news in stories that filled column after column. During the Pullman strike of 1894, Bly's articles stood in marked contrast to those by other journalists, as she portrayed the human side of the strikers struggling for a better existence.

And of course, Bly continued the stunt reporting that had helped make her famous. Her stunts ranged from spending the night in a supposedly haunted house to trying to unmask a psychic as a fraud. Pulitzer had added other stunt girls to his staff by now. They were told to copy Nellie Bly, and they did. For Bly, though, the gimmick of stunts was growing tedious. She tried writing a column for Pulitzer, but it vanished almost as soon as it started.

Meanwhile, competition among New York City's newspapers continued to be fierce. An opportunity to escape her many rivals arose for Bly in Chicago. Publisher James W. Scott had recently taken control of the *Chicago Herald* and merged it with the *Chicago Times.* He was looking for talent. Less than two years after rejoining the *World,* Bly seized the opportunity to sign on with the newly merged *Chicago Times-Herald.*

Again, however, the unpredictable Bly was about to surprise almost everyone. Just five weeks after she started at the *Times-Herald,* Bly quit. Her last story appeared in the newspaper on April 7, 1895. This time, Bly wasn't quitting for another newspaper job. At thirty, Bly had gotten married. Her bridegroom, Robert Livingston Seaman, was a well-known New York businessman, the millionaire owner of the Iron Clad Manufacturing Company and other investments—and an aging man about to turn seventy.

Bly was often complimented on her million-dollar smile. It netted her a millionaire husband in 1895.

TEN

Domestic Life

1895–1914

Once again Bly's name appeared on the pages of the *World.* "Mr. and Mrs. Nellie Bly" blared one headline. According to the *World,* Bly and Seaman had met on a train just days before they wed. They did not immediately announce their marriage, perhaps, as some people speculated, because many of Seaman's relatives suspected Bly of marrying Seaman for his money. Other people thought Bly had suffered a breakup with another man. The pressures of work and a failed relationship had driven her to marrying Seaman.

Whatever the reasons, Bly left Chicago with her husband. She dropped her pen name and began using the name Elizabeth Jane Cochrane Seaman. The couple moved into Seaman's elegant four-story townhouse in New York City. The *World* pointed out that Bly had gained "nearly everything the good fairy of the story book always pictures."

But instead of the good fairy, Mrs. Seaman found her husband's brother Edward, as well as other members of the family, already in residence at the townhouse. Edward Seaman was an alcoholic. He clashed almost immediately with his brother's new wife in a test of wills. Edward was close to his brother and constantly came between the newlyweds in decisions about everything from money to room arrangements within the Seaman residence.

Before long, Bly began to suspect that her husband was having her followed. Wherever she went—out to dinner, to the theater, or just to shop—she felt someone was always watching her. Sometimes she could see a man who appeared to be following her. Bly believed her new husband was spying on her because he was jealous and wanted to prevent her from meeting other men.

One night, Bly suddenly told the driver of her cab to stop. He did, and Bly climbed out. She hurried to a cab that stopped just as suddenly nearby. "Officer," she called to a policeman, "there is a man in that cab who has been following my every movement. I want him arrested." The man in the cab turned out to be one of Robert Seaman's employees.

Several days later, a reporter called at the Seaman residence. Bly took him to meet her husband. "I have no statement to make," Seaman told the reporter. "I don't know that I had any one following her."

"But he swore . . . that you had asked him to follow me," Bly objected as the reporter stood there, taking in the scene.

"I don't ask my servants," Seaman answered. "I direct them what to do."

Perhaps even worse, Bly learned that Seaman had written a will that left only a skimpy fraction of his wealth to her. She had suffered greatly when her father had died without providing for her. She had also seen her mother, whom she was now often supporting, struggle in the past. Bly was just as willful and determined as Robert Seaman. Facing an uncertain financial future, and perhaps unhappy with her current allowance from her husband, she sought out the one source from which she could generate income on her own—the *World.*

An old friend of Bly's from the *World,* Arthur Brisbane, had recently been named the newspaper's Sunday editor. Brisbane quickly set about recruiting a strong staff; Bly was one of the prime candidates on his list. The timing couldn't have been better. By the beginning of 1896, the byline "Nellie Bly" was once again appearing in the pages of the *World.*

Among the first stories Bly covered was the National Woman Suffrage Convention in Washington, D.C. Bly's report included every detail, even descriptions of what the unfashionable suffragettes were wearing. The story took up nearly a full page in the *World.*

Robert Seaman owned a townhouse on this fashionable street.

Bly's interview with Susan B. Anthony, the convention's president, appeared a week later. Bly told her readers that Anthony chided her for mocking the suffragettes' attire. "But I told her," Bly wrote, "if women wanted to succeed they had to go out as women. They had to make themselves as pretty and attractive as possible." Anthony herself followed this credo, Bly pointed out. "She is always gowned richly," Bly wrote, "in style and with most exquisite taste."

The unpredictable Bly was becoming more predictable. Again, and for the last time, she left the *World*. This time her resignation was not given in a huff, but apparently because her husband had chosen to increase the amounts of money she was receiving and would receive upon his death. Among the various holdings Robert Seaman willed to his wife was the Iron Clad Manufacturing Company.

Seemingly at peace with each other after a year of marriage, Mr. and Mrs. Seaman headed for a vacation in Europe. The "vacation" became three years of travel in England, France, Germany, and Italy. Elizabeth Jane Cochrane Seaman managed a more leisurely traveling pace than when she had screamed across Europe as Nellie Bly.

Unfortunately, the Seamans had left incompetent management in charge of the Iron Clad. As news of problems at the factory reached the Seamans, they decided to head back to the United States. Bly left first, because of the unexpected death of her beloved sister Kate from tuberculosis. Kate had been just thirty-two when she died on July 27, 1899. Bly took charge of Kate's daughter Beatrice, who moved into the Seamans' townhouse.

As soon as Robert Seaman arrived in New York, he installed new management at the Iron Clad. The determined and focused Bly also took an active role at the factory. She

The Iron Clad Manufacturing Company made metal wares such as milk cans, garbage cans, and boilers.

learned how to run every machine there and began to invent new equipment to speed the factory's work. Bly's old friend Erasmus Wilson noted Bly's new endeavor in one of his columns. A reader had asked him what had become of Bly. "Oh, she's all right," Wilson wrote. "She's worth about $5 million and has been busying herself with the expert management of her husband's Iron Clad works."

Five years passed. Bly continued to work to improve machinery and systems at the factory. Then, in February 1904, Seaman was struck by a horse and wagon while crossing a street. He suffered a fractured rib. He seemed to recover, but on March 10, he collapsed. The next morning, he died.

The thirty-nine-year-old Bly was now sole owner of Iron Clad. By this time, she held twenty-five patents for inventions that helped the factory run more efficiently. Bly was especially proud of her patent for a steel barrel and began a new company, the American Steel Barrel Company, to produce it.

Bly worked with company manager Edward Gilman to oversee day-to-day business dealings, arriving at her office early in the morning and leaving late each night. And just as Bly always had done, she expertly marketed herself. One of the Iron Clad's promotional cards featured a photo of her declaring her to be "the only woman in the world personally managing Industries of such a magnitude."

Bly also took an active interest in her employees' well-being. At the Iron Clad factory, employees found showers at their disposal as well as a recreation center, bowling alley, and

THE IRON CLAD FACTORIES
ARE THE LARGEST
Of their kind and are owned exclusively
by

❋ **NELLIE BLY** ❋

The only woman in the world
personally managing
Industries of such a magnitude

NATIONAL BOTTLERS' CONVENTION
CLEVELAND, OHIO
OCTOBER 15, 16 and 17, 1901

Bly was over forty when she used this calling card showing her at about age thirty. She liked to look her best always.

library. An on-site hospital and a doctor who made house calls were available. Every December, Bly gave each employee a basket of food that would feed a family of six. No wonder that "The Iron Clad Company boasts that in its fifty years of existence, it has never had a labor trouble of any kind."

Trouble was appearing anyway, however, in the guise of Edward Gilman. After Robert Seaman's death, Bly and Edward Gilman had become not only close business associates but also quite probably more intimate with each other. They went out to dinner together. Sometimes Gilman took Bly sailing on his yacht.

Once Bly took Gilman and Arthur Brisbane for an automobile ride. Brisbane later gave a teasingly exaggerated description of the outing. "Tee hee," he claimed Bly had chortled as she was handed a ticket for speeding. "I don't care." In a note to Bly, Brisbane thanked her for her "kind, courteous and persistent effort to kill me last Saturday."

All the while Bly and Gilman were having fun together, she never seemed to have enough money. Bly couldn't understand why the Iron Clad's cash flow was so poor. She didn't pay attention to the financial end of the business; the company's books were in Gilman's charge. Finally Bly called in independent auditors. They reported that thousands of dollars were missing and probably embezzled. Apparently Gilman had needed cash.

Gilman was indeed responsible for the missing funds. He had given the money to a brother in desperate financial need. "He seemed overcome with remorse," Bly said later. She forgave him. Gilman's admission and Bly's forgiveness, however, did nothing to halt the downward slide of Iron Clad.

Meanwhile, Gilman had begun to grow sick. Diagnosed with stomach cancer, his condition steadily worsened. Bly nursed him as he lay dying in a summer home she owned. It seemed to Bly that a horrifying secret was still locked inside him. "I assured him that no matter what he might have done to injure me, I would freely forgive him," Bly remembered. But Gilman "never gave any answer other than tears." In early 1911, he died.

Gilman could not now be hurt by further investigation into the Iron Clad's books. Determined to understand why the company continued to flounder, Bly ordered another audit. It revealed not only further embezzlement by Gilman but also that two Iron Clad cashiers had been forging Bly's married name on company checks, which they would then cash. The amount stolen ran into hundreds of thousands of dollars.

Although the cashiers were arrested and brought to trial, the theft had taken its toll on Iron Clad. The company was caught in a severe cash crunch. Bills needed to be paid, but the money was not available. Bly frantically tried to raise the needed funds, but she could not produce enough to save Iron Clad. As the company's debts mounted, its creditors filed lawsuit after lawsuit. The Iron Clad was careening toward bankruptcy.

Bly felt she was losing the investment of twelve years of her life. She was outraged that her loss was greater than any penalty imposed on the embezzlers, who had been allowed free on bail. Bly chose not to cooperate with a bankruptcy receiver appointed by the court. When the receiver decided to use Bly's office on Iron Clad property as his own, Bly had the outside stairway to the office—which provided the only convenient access—torn down. And when questioned in court about her company's books and business practices, Bly could not remember or would not divulge many facts. She was charged with contempt of court, fined, and sentenced to twenty days in jail.

*Arthur Brisbane was
a distinguished
journalist and an
untiring supporter
of Bly's.*

Bly never spent time in jail; the judge kept excusing her. Still, the situation was draining her. It was shaping her political opinions, as well. "I learned that the woman who would go into business when there is no such weapon as the ballot to help her along has an orphanlike struggle," she said. ".... I have not heretofore been a suffragette. Now, I am one."

An old friend of Bly's came to the rescue. Arthur Brisbane had moved to the *New York Journal* in 1897. At the *Journal,* he had become the most highly paid editor in America. Brisbane wrote editorials detailing Bly's plight for his readers. In one, he wrote with the capital letters that marked his style: "REMEMBER THAT MEN USUALLY CHEAT WOMEN WHEN THEY GET THE CHANCE .... The case of Nellie Bly."

"HOW WE SAW TEDDY," BY NELLIE BLY AND NELL BRINKLEY
DRAWN BY NELL BRINKLEY AT CHICAGO.

At the Republican National Convention, Bly used a policeman's chest for a writing desk. "This seemed to amuse the crowd," she told readers. "It also amused me."

In addition, Brisbane hired Bly. A little reporting would both distract her and provide some needed income. In June of 1912, he sent her to Chicago to cover the Republican National Convention. Bly couldn't wait to get an interview with the glamorous Teddy Roosevelt. At Bly's request, the illustrator who accompanied her obligingly depicted the middle-aged Bly as a svelte young beauty.

The following February, Brisbane sent Bly to Washington, D.C., to report on a suffrage parade. One gentleman complimented Bly on her outfit and said, "If I could copyright your smile, I could make a million dollars on it." Bly happily quoted him; she was always glad to insert compliments of herself into her stories.

Despite Brisbane's help, Bly's personal assets were quickly dwindling. She tried to protect what property she had

HOW ROOSEVELT LOOKED TO NELLIE BLY

"It was Teddy, the great and only, the glorious and independent and original Teddy! One glance, and he went down the hall in a flying wedge, past that great mass of people, before any of them realized what had occurred.

"One glance at his face, and I felt my heart sink. He was pale. He was tired. He looked worried or unhappy, and as he was rushed down the hall, surrounded by policemen, followed by a bodyguard and led up in the rear by friends, all in a running trot, it was exactly as if he had been put under arrest and was being rushed off a prisoner."—NELLIE BLY.

Bly described Teddy Roosevelt not as a politician, but as a person. He looked tired to her.

left by assigning ownership of it to her mother. The *New York Times* later described Bly's situation, writing, "Luck turned against her . . . and a series of forgeries by her employees, disputes of various sorts . . . and a mass of vexations and costly litigations swallowed up Nellie Bly's fortunes."

Demoralized and exhausted, Bly decided to discuss her situation with another old friend, Oscar Bondy, who was then living in Vienna, Austria. Bondy was a wealthy man and had already helped her financially. Bly got special permission to leave the country while under indictment for contempt of court.

On August 1, 1914, Bly boarded a ship bound for Europe. She expected to be in Vienna for only a few weeks. Her plans would soon change, however. Just days earlier, Austria had declared war against Serbia, triggering the great conflict that would eventually be known as World War I.

Astride a horse, Bly had a good view of the suffrage parade she covered for the Evening Journal.

ELEVEN

A New War

1914–1919

By the time Bly landed in Europe, the continent was smoldering. On June 28, 1914, Archduke Francis Ferdinand, heir to the throne of Austria-Hungary, had been assassinated by a Serb nationalist. Austria-Hungary had retaliated with its declaration of war. Russia mobilized its army to help the Serbs. Then Germany, which had ambitions of extending its reach beyond its existing borders, declared war on Russia. Great Britain and France then declared war on Germany and Austria-Hungary. Smaller countries rushed to take a side, and soon thirty-one countries were battling on either the side of the Allies (which included Great Britain and France) or the Central Powers (which included Germany and Austria-Hungary). As a U.S. citizen, Bly was not involved. The United States remained neutral, letting the European countries fight among themselves.

Once in Vienna, Bly checked into a fashionable hotel not far from the home of Oscar Bondy. Bly could see that Vienna was bustling with preparations for war, its streets crowded with soldiers. Despite the explosive situation in Vienna, as

Bly thought back on her situation at home, she may have felt that her life there was even less secure. Bondy was a warm friend to her. He introduced her to many of his acquaintances, and weeks flew by. Bly's life in the Austrian capital began to seem quite pleasant.

She might have a good reason to make a prolonged stay in Austria if she could get work as a war correspondent. Bly had kept in close contact with Arthur Brisbane at the *New York Evening Journal*. His readers were hungry for war news. Bly worked out an agreement with Brisbane: If she could somehow get to the Eastern Front and write dispatches for Brisbane from the battlefields there, he would publish them with her byline in the *Evening Journal*.

Gaining permission to travel to the front lines was not easy. Bly sought out every contact she could possibly make. She met many notable Austrians, including some of Bondy's influential upper-class friends, who in turn introduced her to the officials who could approve her request. In addition, diplomats and businesspeople from the United States, who were plentiful in Vienna, knew who she was. Many of them did their best to help her.

Finally, in October 1914, Bly got her wish. She and a group of other journalists set out to gain firsthand knowledge of the war. Bly began cabling dispatches back to Brisbane.

Although now age fifty, Bly slogged through the mud of the battlegrounds like any soldier. Her tour took her into the thick of the fighting. During one stop, artillery shells began smashing into the ground near Bly and the other correspondents. The exploding shells sent up sheets of mud that rained down on them.

Readers got an enthralling description of this incident from Bly. "Another frightful explosion," she wrote, ". . . and

As the first woman war correspondent at the Eastern Front, Bly conveyed the war's ravages to readers back home in the United States. Below, she visits with an Austrian general.

one after the other six shells fell and buried themselves in the same soft earth. Then I got into the trench. Two hundred feet was near enough for me. I was not afraid. I could not run. Yet my mind was busy. I thought another shot would follow. It will doubtless be better aimed. If it is, we shall die."

Bly's tour lasted a month. All the dispatches she and the other war correspondents wrote were carefully read and censored by the Austrian authorities before being cabled out of the country. If vital military information had been included, it was eliminated. And if a story criticized the Austrian war effort, the offending sentences were cut. Sometimes censors destroyed an entire article.

Bly's dispatches were lightly censored, but most of what she wrote passed inspection easily—not surprising, since Bly clearly favored Austrian positions. News coming into Austria-Hungary was just as heavily censored as news leaving the country, so Bly worked in the dark about many events abroad. The news she heard had an Austrian point of view. And Bly was predisposed to side with Austria-Hungary, since she harbored a keen dislike of its enemy Great Britain. Arthur Brisbane and William Randolph Hearst shared Bly's disdain for the British, and the *Evening Journal* readily published stories with a pro-Austrian slant.

In May 1915, a German submarine attacked the British passenger liner *Lusitania*. Torpedoes ripped through the ship's hull, sinking it and killing more than a thousand people, including 128 U.S. citizens. The deaths of these U.S. citizens—mostly women and children—turned public sentiment in the U.S. against Germany and Austria.

Bly was unaware, however, of the sinking of the *Lusitania*. She continued her pro-Austrian efforts. When her tour of the front line ended, she attempted to organize food

Bly loved Austria and its people. For this reason, she misunderstood American sentiment against Austria and its allies during World War I.

drives for the benefit of Austrians made hungry due to the war. She sent pleas for aid back to Brisbane and Hearst. Despite the German attack on the *Lusitania,* they readily publicized her pleas.

Bly pressed on with a fund-raising drive for Austria's widows and orphans. She encouraged her U.S. readers to send silver quarters to Austria. In return, she would ensure that contributors' names were placed in a permanent record called the "Gold Book." In addition, Bly wrote a postcard to her old friend in Pittsburgh, Erasmus Wilson, asking him to solicit contributions through his column. "Ask your readers to send 15 cts and their names to me," she told him. She signed the card, "Your Kid Nellie Bly."

The course of public sentiment in the U.S., meanwhile, continued its shift against the Central Powers. In 1917, U.S. President Woodrow Wilson learned of a German plot against the United States. Germany was trying to convince Mexico to enter the war as an ally of the Central Powers. In return, Germany would help Mexico regain territory that Mexico had once controlled but lost to the United States. U.S. citizens were outraged. Even more galvanizing was the sinking of several unarmed U.S. merchant ships by the Germans. Wilson had had enough. On April 6, 1917, he declared the United States to be at war with Germany.

Having aligned itself with Germany, Austria was drawn into the confrontation with the United States. Bly was an enemy alien. Her dispatches ended, and *Evening Journal* readers heard no more from her.

After the U.S. entered the war against the Central Powers, U.S. citizens in Austria could not travel within the country without special permission. Because of Bly's pro-Austrian views, however, she easily gained permission to travel. She made the most of it, touring museums, going to auctions, and in general enjoying herself as a tourist. She proudly wore one piece of jewelry wherever she went—a small pin in the shape of the American flag.

In the fall of 1918, a year-and-a-half after the United States had joined the fight, World War I came to an end. The Allies had defeated the Central Powers. Bly decided to return to the United States. She boarded a train to Switzerland, which had remained neutral throughout the war. She then continued on to Paris, where she applied for a visa to return home.

Unfortunately, Bly's home wasn't sure it wanted her back. The U.S. government was naturally suspicious of Bly. After many interviews with Bly, U.S. authorities decided that Austrian censorship had probably kept Bly ignorant of the American perspective on the war. In 1919, Bly was allowed to return to the United States.

By that time, the contempt of court charge against Bly had been dropped. But her business affairs were in a shambles. Bly's mother and her brother Albert had effectively taken control of the few financial assets Bly had remaining. One of these was the American Steel Barrel Company. The company was one of the last possessions Bly had hoped to retain. Albert had cared for Mary Jane while Bly was in Europe. He had schemed to gain control of the company while his sister was away and convinced their elderly mother, who was increasingly fragile, to back him up.

"My Dear Q. O.," Bly wrote to Erasmus Wilson in March 1919, "I returned . . . to find my mother whom I cared for so tenderly since my early youth is under the evil influences of my brother Albert." Bly told Wilson that Mary Jane was claiming ownership of all Bly's property. Bly's net worth, Bly wrote, was "$3.65 and a trunk full of Paris evening dresses."

Back in New York City, Bly found she was not welcome at the home Albert and Mary Jane shared. Bly moved in with her brother Harry. She needed work, and once again Arthur Brisbane stepped in. Would Bly accept a position at the *Evening Journal* as an editorial page columnist?

Bly had years of reporting experience behind her. She had blazed her way through dramatic and sometimes frightening stunts. She had bravely reported scenes from a deadly international conflict. Even so, Bly's pay at the *Evening Journal* would be a fraction of what she had earned years earlier.

Bly was in no position to argue. She accepted Brisbane's well-intentioned offer.

Bly, right, *stands with a young mother and children—one of many needy families Bly sought to help through her column.*

TWELVE

Brief Shining Star

1919–1922

In the past few years, Bly's lustrous dark hair had dulled and grayed. Her tiny waist had broadened; her trim figure had become matronly.

Also changed was the newspaper world to which Bly returned. When Bly had last been on a newspaper staff, she had been one of a few maverick women. Now, many of the aggressive reporters around her were women. And while the youthful Bly had been an innovator in the techniques of stunt reporting, stunt reporting was now considered outmoded, even quaint. Bly was a journalistic dinosaur verging on extinction.

Still, the "Nellie Bly" byline managed to recapture the public's attention. With the *Evening Journal* as a channel for funneling ideas to readers, Bly took up a number of causes. She advocated abolishing the death penalty. She wrote about the needs of the homeless, of the blind, and of unwed mothers.

But it was the cause of needy children, especially orphans, that Bly particularly promoted. She attempted to make the lives of such youngsters happier as best she could. In June 1920, she treated 750 orphans to an outing at the city's famous amusement park, Coney Island. Perhaps more importantly, through her column, Bly arranged for the adoption of many abandoned and orphaned children, children who, as Arthur Brisbane put it, "had no other claim upon her except the fact that they were poor and friendless."

One of the young orphans Bly helped was the daughter of a woman Bly had written about in one of her columns. The girl's name was Dorothy Harris; her mother had been a drug addict and thief. Bly's heart went out to the little six-year-old. She gained guardianship of the child and then set about trying to find a suitable family to take Dorothy permanently.

Bly continued to cover the news as a reporter. She covered the 1920 Republican National Convention in Chicago for the *Evening Journal.* That same year, women won the right to vote through passage of the Nineteenth Amendment to the U.S. Constitution.

On February 16, 1921, Bly's mother, Mary Jane, died of bladder cancer at the age of ninety-four. In Bly's columns, Bly often referred to herself as "grievously wronged." But she did not reveal much more to her readers about her feelings for her mother. "If you would be great," she wrote, "two things are of ultimate importance. The first is to know yourself. The second is not to let the world know you."

Bly herself was frequently ill. Her energy had been sapped by so many years of work and stress. She was in and out of hospitals throughout 1921, suffering from exhaustion. During the same period, more and more letters poured in from people asking for her help—unwed mothers, widows left with young children, men needing jobs. Bly hired a crew of secretaries to help her answer each plea.

On January 9, 1922, Bly's column in the *New York Evening Journal* ran for the last time. That day, she was admitted to New York City's St. Mark's Hospital with a severe case of bronchopneumonia. Eighteen days later, on January 27, Bly died. She was fifty-seven.

Bly probably would have been proud of the public response. The major New York City newspapers featured her exploits in her obituary. The *New York Times* also noted, in a later report, that her estate was valued at just nine thousand dollars.

The *World* printed a one-column obituary. It mentioned Bly's noteworthy stories, including the Blackwell's Island exposé and Bly's account of her trip around the world. Arthur Brisbane provided a fuller account in the *Evening Journal.* "Nellie Bly was at one time, after the death of her husband, a rich woman, worth millions," Brisbane recalled. "In short order business men managed to treat her, as women are usually treated by their masculine 'friends,' and she had nothing." But whatever Bly's troubles had been, Brisbane continued, she was "the best reporter in America."

Both as a journalist and as a human being, Bly had been a complicated figure. She had a strong desire to make the world a better place, especially for needy women and children. She was often outraged at the petty—and sometimes not-so-petty—injustices of the nineteenth century. She was driven to do good with a belief that whatever the circumstances, she would prevail. She possessed an immense ego that aided her in getting the story. But that ego also, more than once, led to personal downfalls.

The woman who had streaked around the world to thunderous applause and helped to pioneer a new brand of journalism was buried in a grave that remained unmarked for fifty years. But that was just the last contradiction in a life that had held many, for Bly's legend lingers on. She worked as a

In her colorful life, Bly dazzled thousands of people, lost millions of dollars, and left her stamp on American journalism forever.

full-time reporter for relatively few years. Yet Bly had an impact on American journalism that is still felt. An 1889 verse written about Bly perhaps best summed up the intense burst of light that was her life:

> *I wonder when they'll send a girl*
> *to travel around the sky.*
> *Read the answer in the stars,*
> *they wait for Nellie Bly.*

Sources

p. 9   *New York World,* July 15, 1894.

p. 9   Sidney Lens, *The Labor Wars: From the Molly Macguires to the Sit Downs* (New York: Doubleday & Company, Inc., 1973), 85–86.

p. 9   *New York World,* July 15, 1894.

p. 10   *New York World,* July 11, 1894.

p. 10   Ibid.

p. 11   *New York World,* July 15, 1894.

p. 13   Brooke Kroeger, *Nellie Bly: Daredevil, Reporter, Feminist* (New York: Random House, 1994), 5.

p. 16   from Nellie Bly's testimony at her mother's divorce proceedings, as cited in Kroeger, *Nellie Bly,* 20.

p. 17   Ibid.

p. 21   *The American Experience,* "Around the World in 72 Days," program transcript (PBS/WGBH), 3.

p. 22   *Pittsburg Dispatch,* January 14, 1885.

pp. 23–24   *Pittsburg Dispatch,* February 3, 1885.

p. 24   *Pittsburg Dispatch,* January 17, 1885.

p. 24   *Pittsburg Commercial Gazette,* January 25, 1890.

p. 24   *Pittsburg Dispatch,* January 17, 1885.

p. 25   *Pittsburg Dispatch,* January 25, 1885.

p. 25   *Pittsburg Commercial Gazette,* January 25, 1890.

pp. 25–26   *Pittsburg Dispatch,* January 25, 1885.

p. 27   *Pittsburg Commercial Gazette,* January 25, 1890.

p. 28   *Pittsburg Dispatch,* February 8, 1885.

p. 29   *Pittsburg Dispatch,* October 17, 1885.

p. 29   Nellie Bly, *Six Months in Mexico* (New York: John W. Lovell, 1886), 5.

p. 29   Ibid.

p. 30   *Pittsburg Dispatch,* February 21, 1886.

p. 32   Ibid.

p. 33   Bly, *Six Months in Mexico,* 150.

p. 33   *Pittsburg Dispatch,* March 7, 1886.

p. 33   Ibid.

p. 33   Bly, *Six Months in Mexico,* 199.

p. 34   *Pittsburg Dispatch,* June 23, 1886.

p. 35   *Pittsburg Dispatch,* August 1, 1886.

p. 35   *Pittsburg Commercial Gazette,* January 25, 1890.

p. 38   Nellie Bly, *Godey's Lady's Book,* January 1889, 20.

p. 42   Nellie Bly, *Ten Days in a Mad-House* (New York: Norman L. Munro, 1887), 6.

p. 42   Ibid., 9.

p. 43   Ibid., 17.

p. 43   *New York Times,* September 26, 1887.

pp. 44–45   Bly, *Ten Days in a Mad-House,* 27.

p. 45   Ibid., 52.

p. 45   Ibid., 93.

p. 45   Ibid., 76.

p. 46   *New York Evening Sun,* October 14, 1887.

p. 46   Bly, *Ten Days in a Mad-House,* 98.

p. 46   *New York Mail and Express,* August 27, 1887.

p. 49   Nellie Bly, *Nellie Bly's Book: Around the World in Seventy-Two Days* (New York: The Pictorial Weeklies Co., 1890), 3.

p. 50   *New York World,* August 12, 1888.

p. 50   Bly, *Nellie Bly's Book,* 4.

pp. 50–51   Ibid., 5.

p. 51   Ibid., 6.

p. 51   Ibid., 10.

p. 52   Ibid., 17.

p. 55   *New York World,* November 14, 1889.

p. 55   Bly, *Nellie Bly's Book,* 18.

p. 55   Ibid., 19.

p. 57   Ibid., 20.

p. 57   Ibid., 45.

pp. 58–59   *The Journalist,* November 30, 1889.

p. 60   Bly, *Nellie Bly's Book,* 167.

p. 61   Ibid., 192.

p. 61   Ibid.

p. 61   Ibid., 193.

p. 63   Ibid., 194.

pp. 63–64   Ibid., 261.

p. 64   Ibid., 263.

pp. 64–65   Ibid., 266-267.

p. 65   Ibid., 280.

p. 67   *New York World,* January 26, 1890.

p. 67   *New York Times,* January 26, 1890.

p. 68   *New York World,* January 26, 1890.

p. 68   Ibid.

pp. 70–71   Ibid.

p. 72   Bly, *Nellie Bly's Book,* 277.

p. 73   Ibid., 280.

p. 75   *New York World,* January 26, 1890.

p. 76   Ibid.

p. 76   Ibid.

p. 77   Ibid.

p. 77   *The Metropolis,* as quoted in *The Journalist,* February 1, 1890.

p. 77   *The Journalist,* February 1, 1890.

p. 77   Ibid.

p. 78   *The Journalist,* December 19, 1891.

p. 79   Nellie Bly, letter to Erasmus Wilson, August 22, 1890.

p. 79   *The Journalist,* August 20, 1891.

p. 79   *The Journalist,* October 8, 1892.

p. 80   Nellie Bly, letter to Erasmus Wilson, January 26, 1891.

p. 80   Nellie Bly, letter to Erasmus Wilson, March 9, 1891.

p. 80   *The Journalist,* February 6, 1892.

p. 80   *New York World,* September 17, 1893.

p. 83   *New York World,* April 21, 1895.

p. 83   Ibid.

p. 84   *New York Recorder,* November 11, 1895.

p. 86   *New York World,* February 2, 1896.

p. 87   *Pittsburgh Gazette-Times,* May 16, 1906.

p. 88   Promotional card, National Bottlers' Convention, 1901.

p. 89   *Brooklyn Eagle,* December 24, 1905.

p. 89   Arthur Brisbane, letter to Nellie Bly, June 26, 1907, Brisbane Family Papers, as cited in Kroeger, *Nellie Bly,* 315.

p. 89   *New York Times,* January 20, 1912.

p. 90   Ibid.

p. 91   *New York Times,* January 28, 1912.

p. 91   *New York Evening Journal,* July 7, 1911.

p. 92   *New York Evening Journal,* March 3, 1913.

p. 93   *New York Times,* June 28, 1911.

p. 96   *New York Evening Journal,* December 8, 1914.

p. 99   Nellie Bly, postcard to Erasmus Wilson, August 21, 1915.

p. 101   Nellie Bly, letter to Erasmus Wilson, March 1919.

p. 103   *New York Evening Journal,* October 12, 1921.

p. 104   *New York Evening Journal,* November 6, 1919.

p. 105   *New York Evening Journal,* January 28, 1922.

p. 106   As quoted in the *Los Angeles Times,* March 28, 1994.

Bibliography

Books by Nellie Bly

The Mystery of Central Park. New York: G.W. Dillingham, 1889.
Nellie Bly's Book: Around the World in Seventy-Two Days. New York: The
    Pictorial Weeklies Co., 1890.
Six Months in Mexico. New York: John W. Lovell, 1886.
Ten Days in a Mad-House. New York: Norman L. Munro, 1887.

Further Reading

Bates, J. Douglas. *The Pulitzer Prize: The Inside Story of America's Most
    Prestigious Award.* New York: Carol Publishing Group, 1991.
Kroeger, Brooke. *Nellie Bly: Daredevil, Reporter, Feminist.* New York: Times
    Books, Random House, 1994.
Kurtz, Howard. *Media Circus: The Trouble with America's Newspapers.* New
    York: New York Times Books, 1993.
Lens, Sidney. *The Labor Wars: From the Molly Macguires to the Sit Downs.*
    New York: Doubleday & Company, Inc., 1973.
Milton, Joyce. *The Yellow Kids: Foreign Correspondents in the Heyday of Yellow
    Journalism.* New York: Harper & Row, 1989.
Schilpp, Madelon Golden and Sharon M. Murphy. *Great Women of the Press.*
    Carbondale: Southern Illinois Press, 1983.

Index

Photo Acknowledgments

Photographs have been reproduced with permission from: Brown Brothers,
pp. 6, 23, 105, 106; General Research Division, The New York Public Library,
Astor, Lenox and Tilden Foundations, pp. 11, 62; The Apollo Memorial
Library, p. 12; © Museum of the City of New York, pp. 17, 79, 82; Special
Collections, University Library, Indiana University of Pennsylvania, Indiana,
Pennsylvania, p. 18; Slater Mill Historic Site, Pawtucket, Rhode Island, p. 20;
Carnegie Library, Pittsburgh, pp. 26, 86, 87, 88; Foster Hall Collection, Center
for American Music, University of Pittsburgh Library System, p. 27; The
Library of Congress, pp. 30 (microfilm #1863), 56 (neg. #LC USZ62-59924),
65 (Lot 6620, #429), 91 (neg #USZ62-29540-812352); Al Greene/Archive
Photos, p. 34 (left); Culver Pictures, pp. 34 (right), 66; Corbis-Bettmann,
pp. 36, 44, 74, 97 (top); Independent Picture Service, p. 41; Archive Photos,
pp. 39, 48; Corbis, pp. 53, 70, 72; © Collection of the New-York Historical
Society, pp. 54, 54–55, 85; The Library of Congress, Detroit Publishing Co.
Photograph Collection, pp. 58 (neg. #LC-D4-22337-DLC), 69
(neg. #LC-D4-9176-DLC); The National Railway Museum/Science & Society
Picture Library, p. 60; UPI/Corbis-Bettmann, pp. 2, 76, 97 (bottom), 99, 102;
Harry Ransom Humanities Resource Center, University of Texas-Austin,
pp. 92, 93, 94.

Cover: Corbis-Bettmann